The Project 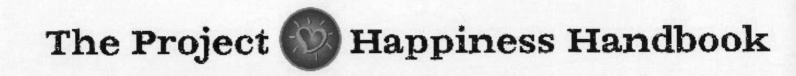 Happiness Handbook

By Randy Taran and Maria Lineger
Graphics by Ruben Nunez

Inspired by the students & teachers from Mount Madonna School (United States)
Tibetan Children's Village (India)
Creative Minds International Academy (Nigeria)
Dominion Heritage Academy (Nigeria)

To everyone who hopes for more happiness.

Waves of Appreciation

Special thanks to His Holiness the XIV Dalai Lama for his participation in Project Happiness and for his universal perspective which inspires us all. We are grateful to the Dalai Lama Foundation for their help and kindness at every stage. Special thanks to David Taran who has been a longtime supporter of The Project Happiness Handbook and greater project in so many ways.

We'd like to thank the teachers and all of the students from our three cornerstone schools in California, Nigeria, and India. Special thanks to Ward Mailliard for his contribution and commitment, Emmanuel Ande Ivorgba and Yeshi Khando for their fresh viewpoints. We are grateful to Sri Sridharan for connecting us all together and the students who really helped inspire and create The Project Happiness Handbook: Yolanda Diaz, Daniel Nanas, Mark Hansen, Tom Shani, Devin Bhattacharya and Emily Crubach, as well as Shannon Frediani, Emily's mother for sharing her reflections as a parent.

We extend our thanks to our special contributors: Angeles Arrien, Beck Institute for Cognitive Therapy and Research, Bunthouen Hack, Carol Dweck, Fred Luskin, Gordon Training International, Kristen Neff, Martin Seligman, Masaru Emoto, Richard Davidson, Robert Assagioli, Sobonfu Some, Tal Ben Shahar, The Center for Contemplative Mind in Society, The Center for Nonviolent Communication, Tom Brown, Jr. and 6 Seconds. Each one introduces a meaningful and unique perspective to the book.

We appreciate the kindness of George Lucas, Richard Davidson, Richard Gere, Adam Yauch, Nirmala Deshpandi, Ambassador Mulford and former President of India, Abdul Kalam, who shared their insights in interviews for Project Happiness.

In the area of design and visuals, we are grateful to Ruben Nunez, Jack Schaub, Shmuel Thaler and Amanda Sargenti. John Sorensen encapsulated the journey in film and his special relationship with the students and project is much appreciated.

Thank you to our educational consultant and dear friend Marsha Clark, digital mediator Jim "Sky" Schuyler and our diligent reviewers Miriam von Guggenberg, Laura Delizonna, and Liane Moneta. Our Youth Advisory Board provided a fresh perspective - special thanks to Miriam von Guggenberg, Zoe Taran and other members of the team.

Thanks also to Dana Cappiello, Erik Stangvik, Leslie Haas, Julia Reigel, Melissa Hollatz, Jeff Ulin and Kimya Lashgari.

Finally, we are grateful to our families, who have also been on this journey, for showing us the real meaning of happiness in moments cherished.

The last wave is for you - yeah, the you who's reading this - for all the ways you can discover happiness and then spread it around...

This book is NOT....

A textbook
Religious
A quick recipe for happiness
Going to happen overnight
Easy
Going to kill you
Pointless
A competition

It's not anything but an invitation!

You are not a product
We're not going to give you the answers
It's all up to you

Yeah, the Change Starts Now!

Stressed? Bored? Angry? Think there's something missing in your life? This book may have come to you at the perfect moment. Life can be full of stress! As a group of recent graduates, we understand that it's hard to care about certain things, especially when it's difficult to relate them to your own life. We all have different priorities in our lives... is happiness one of them? This handbook can help you make happiness your priority!

Give yourself a chance to discover what you have in common with the ideas and stories in this handbook. We don't want to change you - we want to inspire you and remind you that you can find out a lot about yourself and the choices you have. We're not saying this handbook will definitely change your life - but it just might... if you allow it.

It All Started Here...

Tibetan Children's Village (TCV)
Dharamsala, India

Mount Madonna School
Watsonville, California

Dominion Heritage Academy Jos
Nigeria

How It All Started...

Project Happiness started when we met other high school seniors from different countries to explore real happiness. We came together from the United States, India, and Nigeria to have a conversation…first online, then face-to-face, which you can watch for yourself in our documentary film (www.projecthappiness.com). Through our conversations, we realized that we all have our own views of what happiness means to us, many similar and some very different.

Among all these different views, is there actually one definition of happiness that we can all agree on?

We decided it would help to explore even further and ask some interesting individuals to shed some light on this question. So, we asked George Lucas (filmmaker & Star Wars creator), Richard Gere (actor & humanitarian), Richard Davidson (world renowned neuroscientist), and Adam Yauch (Beastie Boys musician). Then we went to India to visit Ghandi's orphanage where we had a chance to speak with Nirmala Desphande (carrier of Gandhi's legacy). Finally, we gathered together with our international friends to speak with someone who we thought might really have some answers for us…Nobel Peace Prize Winner, the Dalai Lama.

Here is what we learned...

1. No one is the expert on your happiness…except you. For this reason, no one else can define it for you.
2. What we do have in common is that we ALL want more happiness in our lives…and less struggle.
3. Meeting cool people and traveling to exotic places are great, but you don't need to travel across the globe to figure out what happiness means to you. You just need to look within yourself.

The real journey is within and yours starts now!

The First Meeting
Dharamsala, India

1st Row - Tsechoe Wang Mo, Tenzin Dhanzay, Mercy Bisi, Nina Castanon, Tenzin Youdon, Naomi Magid, Yangchen Dolma, Lhamo Dolma, Dechen Lhadon.

2nd Row - Alexander Crawford, Ngawang Paljor, John Nuri-Vissel, Jeremy Thweatt

3rd Row - Dorji Gyalsten, Prabha Sharan, Mark Hansen, Emily Crubaugh, Kristen van't Rood, Tsering Diki, Tenzin Nyidon, Daniel Nanas, Emmanuel Ivorgba

4th Row - Palden Namgyal, Luke Sander-Self, Tenzin Choempel, Tenzin Dawa, Jonji Barbes Tenzin Peme, Tenzin, Tom Shani, Madeline Weston Miles, Faith Ozoh, Tenzin Yonten, Tenzin Dhazay

Getting Started...

Who is this handbook for?

Whether you've picked up this book out of curiosity or your teacher was inspired by the opportunity, it doesn't matter. Use it on your own, use it in your class, with your friends, or even try it with your family. Most importantly, use it in ways that are meaningful to you!

What's in this handbook?

This handbook was inspired by our own year-long journey. In it you will find seven chapters based on themes that were most meaningful to us. Within each chapter, you'll come across lots of ideas and activities to help you explore who you are and what makes you happy. For example, you'll read about our thoughts along our journey, quotes from the people we interviewed, things you can apply to your own life from leading thinkers, cross-cultural stories and plenty of space to write what's going on for you. It's a mix of practical tools, inspiring ideas, and space to reflect.

How do I use this handbook?

Be creative and use it your way. Think of it as a journal. Try anything that lets you express what's real for you, whether it's writing, creating poetry, rap, or art. Don't just write what you think someone else wants you to say, or what you're "supposed" to say. Write what makes sense to you. Neatness and grammar are not priorities here, your ideas are…and so is your happiness.

This book is an experience not just another textbook to dust off.

Table of Contents

Chapter I	Happiness	1
Chapter II	Obstacles to Happiness	17
Chapter III	Self-Reflection	39
Chapter IV	Self-Mastery	69
Chapter V	Compassion in Action	107
Chapter VI	Interdependence	137
Chapter VII	Share your Gifts	159

Making it Mine

Exploring the Ideas	4	Tracking My Happiness	11	Exploring my Community	14
The Purpose of this Book	6	Does Happiness Change?	12	What do I NOW know about happiness?	16
My Story	21	Which Direction to Paddle	29	My Defining Moments	35
Reflecting on Struggle	25	Reflecting on Cause and Effect	31	What do I NOW know about happiness?	37
Where I choose to hang out	27	Reflecting on Other's Suffering	33		
Who am I?	41	Who's Playing in My Jungle?	49	My Inner Guidance System	61
How I See Myself	42	Reflecting on My Mindset	51	The Guest House	62
The Boomerang Effect	43	Training My Brain	53	Tracking My Four Rivers	64
My Wheels in Motion	45	Reflecting on My Responses	55	Ideas about My Gift	67
Get Your Tickets	47	Mental Test Drive	58	What do I NOW know about happiness?	68
Aikido	70	Pushing My Buttons	82	My Zone of Peace	94
Creating My Own Recipe	73	Training Sessions	84	Reflecting on My Armor	96
Finding My Will	76	Reflecting on Guilt	88	An Open Mind and Heart	99
Reflecting on My World	79	Self-Compassion	90	Waves of Appreciation	104
The Positive Power of Words	80	My Nourishment Plan	92	What do I NOW know about happiness?	106
Checking out Connections	110	Reflecting on My Self-Compassion	120	Reflecting on My View of Others	128
Reflecting on Compassion	113	What Self-Compassion IS	121	What's Your Plan?	130
Reflecting on Genuine Compassion	116	Packing for the Ride	123	Rewriting My Story	135
How full is your cup?	119	Tracking My Conversations	126	What do I NOW know about happiness?	136
Reflecting on My Interactions	140	My Relationship with the Planet	149	Our Ecological Footprint	155
Tracking my Inner Workings	144	Roles we Play	152	Exploring My Part	157
Interdependence With Others!	145	The Journey of our Jeans	153	What do I NOW know about happiness?	158
Checking out My Interactions	146	The Perils of Plastic	154		
My Own Happiness	162	Finding My Piece	166	My Path to Happiness	176
My Own and Others' Happiness	165	Finding My Path	168	My Credo	177

I

HAPPINESS

"For my part, meeting innumerable others from all over the world and from every walk of life reminds me of our **basic sameness as human beings.**

Indeed, the more I see of the world, the clearer it becomes that **no matter what our situation,** whether we are rich or poor, educated or not, of one race, gender, religion or another, we all desire to be **happy and to avoid suffering."**

-The XIV Dalai Lama

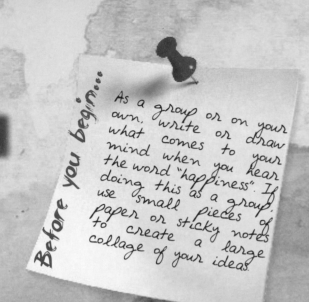

Before you begin... As a group or on your own, write or draw what comes to your mind when you hear the word "happiness". If doing this as a group, use small pieces of paper or sticky notes to create a large collage of your ideas.

As human beings, we all seek happiness.

While this is a simple statement, finding lasting happiness is not so easy. To begin with, what we do share is the desire to avoid painful experiences and to look for ways to bring happiness into our lives. What we do not share with one another is a common understanding of happiness. What makes one person happy may not be the same for another because each of our characters and preferences are unique, and we also come from different families, communities and cultures. At the end of the day, we must all create our own individual definition of happiness.

WHAT IS HAPPINESS?

We can think of happiness in several ways. We often feel happy when we fulfill our needs and desires. This includes:

- → Meeting basic needs
- → Tending to our comfort
- → Getting what we want
- → Experiencing pleasure
- → Achieving short-term goals

Although meeting our needs and desires can give us feelings that are often quite pleasurable, they tend to be short-term and eventually fade. We feel our mind and senses responding to that pleasure or comfort and we call it happiness. Sometimes we might have an extreme craving for something sweet (e.g., chocolate, ice cream, soda). Once we satisfy that craving, we might feel blissful, but this feeling is temporary. Soon, the craving returns. Then there's the exhilaration we feel when buying or receiving a gift that has occupied our wish list for a long time (e.g., new shoes, favorite music, the latest technology).

After the pleasure of having this object fades, we desire something else. The idea here is that happiness, which depends on external objects or attainment of immediate desires, will only bring temporary satisfaction. Then, when we find ourselves wanting something new, which we often do, we repeat the process. We end up creating a never-ending cycle as we constantly search for more objects and increasingly intense experiences that satisfy us temporarily.

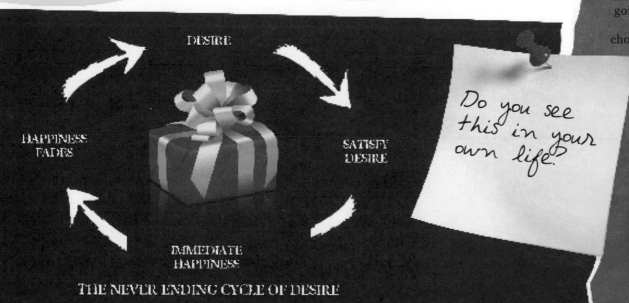

DESIRE

SATISFY DESIRE

IMMEDIATE HAPPINESS

HAPPINESS FADES

THE NEVER ENDING CYCLE OF DESIRE

Do you see this in your own life?

"Pleasure is addictive. Joy could be addictive, too. It's a biological response. When you get in the car, you press on the pleasure pedal, but you have a choice.

You can choose joy and toodle along at 35 miles an hour. You're going to be able to go around the world a hundred times. If you choose the nitrous oxide pleasure pedal, you'll push it as hard as you can, full-bore at 300 miles an hour; but you're only going to go about a half a mile."

What ride do you take?

Exploring the Ideas

Using the space below, identify a variety of things (objects, people, experiences, etc.) in your life that make you happy. You can make a list, write freely, sketch, rap... whatever inspires you! Which things have brought you short-term happiness? Which have brought you long-term happiness? What's the difference between short-term and long-term happiness? How would you define them? What are the benefits of both? If you are in a group, share your ideas and come up with a group definition for short and long-term happiness.

Short-Term Happiness
Characteristics:

Benefits:

Definition:

Long-Term Happiness
Characteristics:

Benefits:

Definition:

Why is happiness is so important?
DORJI
India

Can you think of a time when you've experienced happiness that's come from within?
DANIEL
USA

Please, can any of you share your experience with me on how my actions can be motivated by concern for others?
PATIENCE
Nigeria

What destroys your happiness?
DONGBU
India

What do you say to someone looking for happiness with a materialistic motivation, Do you confront them and tell them that they are wrong to do so or let them continue?
NINA
USA

Questions I have...

What is sadness' place in achieving happiness?
JONJI
USA

Our Journey Begins

Mount Madonna School

We've just found out that we'll be working on our project in conjunction with groups from the Tibetan Children's Village in India and from the Dominion Heritage Academia in Nigeria. The members of my class and I are in the process of signing up for an e-mail group, where we can write a message and have it forwarded to everyone who's working with us in different countries. In order to get to know each other better, we've been asking questions that relate to the project. The following questions are taken from e-mails that were written by either the Tibetan students from India, Nigerian students, or American students.

Our Journey

Hi, everyone. Today we are talking about a very difficult topic: happiness. What we are finding is that happiness in our life is a very difficult thing to be found. I say I am happy now, but it will change as soon as my mood and desires change.
DONGBU

I really don't know what happiness is. There are times when I have felt happy but I am confused about true happiness. I know that when I felt happy it was because of others and not something I did myself. I also know that when I am sad it is usually something I have done myself. And I know that after I feel happy I feel sadder than before.
KRISTEN

Happiness is a universal and fundamental desire of all humans. I see this clearly in my life and in the lives of others around me. This is a truth for all times and places.
PATIENCE

The purpose of this book...

is to explore the idea of real and lasting happiness that remains with us regardless of the circumstances around us. When thinking of how we can create this kind of happiness, we need to know what makes us happy in the long run, as well as what gives us pleasure in the now. Many people who have all the basic needs of life, such as food, housing, and family, still experience suffering, such as the presence of anxiety, stress, and depression.

What makes us genuinely happy?

We can begin by thinking of where our ideas of happiness come from. Where do YOURS come from? Underneath each person, write what you think THEY want for YOUR happiness.

FAMILY

FRIENDS

COMMUNITY

MEDIA

What creates lasting happiness?
This is the central question...

When we began our inquiry into what was happiness, we interviewed and discussed the question with a variety of people, including politicians, celebrities, and students in other countries. Here is what a few of them had to say.

"I think happiness can never be defined in short and concise words; it is a vast concept. Happiness is inner peace of mind which one can neither buy from the market nor snatch from someone else."
TSERING
Student, Tibetan Children's Village, India

"Happiness for me comes from different places. Some of the places of happiness include knowing who I am, that I have a community to count on, and knowing that there are myths and mysteries out there to explore that I can make a part of my life."
SOBONFU SOME
Indigenous wisdom carrier and author

"The reality is, we can change. We can change ourselves. We can change our minds. We can change our hearts. And therefore the universe changes...my mind and my heart can achieve a certain level of development that then my outer reality reflects my inner reality."
RICHARD GERE
Humanitarian & Actor

Dear Kristen,
Hi, I am happy to know that you are curious about true happiness and I am also in search of true happiness. For me, I feel true happiness lies inside our soul. If we are happy inward, naturally we feel healthy and happy.
LHAMO

"Is happiness inborn?" We have heard many of our scholars commenting on happiness. But I still don't know what makes us happy. I am happy when I am satisfied, but I will not be satisfied forever. What do you think?
TENZIN

Our teacher, Mr. Mailliard asked us a question about the project. It was something along the lines of what we wanted to get out of the project. I realize that I care a lot more about the process of making this book than the actual end result.
What I mean is that I am more excited to work with all of you and share ideas along the way than about what the final cut will look like.

JOHN-NURI

Perspective Matters

Sometimes how we see the world affects how happy we are in it…

Once upon a time in a small village, a poor unfortunate man lived with his mother, his wife, and his six children in a little one-room hut. Because they were so crowded, the hut was full of crying and quarreling. One day, when man couldn't stand it anymore, he ran to the Rabbi for advice.

The Rabbi said that he should go home and put five chickens, a rooster, and a goose in the hut to live with his family. The poor man hurried home, took the animals out of the shed, and brought them into his little hut. A week went by, and there was the usual quarreling and crying and honking, crowing, and clucking. He went back to the Rabbi again. The Rabbi told him to bring a goat inside the house to live with him. Shocked, the man went home and did as the Rabbi said. Life continued to get worse for the man, and the hut seemed to be smaller by the day. Frustrated, he ran to the Rabbi, begging for his help. The Rabbi told the man to bring a cow into the house. The man trudged home and took the cow into his hut.

The Boomerang Effect

Have you ever thrown a boomerang? Unlike a ball or Frisbee, it actually comes back to you. Our thoughts are the same. We put our thoughts out into the world, and the results of these thoughts often come back into our lives. Have you ever noticed how thoughts can become words, words can become actions, actions can become habits, and so on? We might want to watch our thoughts with care.

What thoughts are you putting out into the world? What has been coming back into your life?

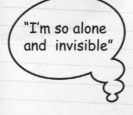
"I'm so alone and invisible"

"I have reliable friends"

"Life's pretty good right now"

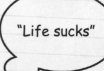
"Life sucks"

What you focus on often comes back into your life.
Your thoughts are like boomerangs.

See It to Believe It?

Our thoughts do influence our environment - even water!

Dr. Masaru Emoto, a Japanese researcher tested this statement when he conducted a water crystal experiment. He exposed water in glasses to different words, pictures, or music and then froze and examined the water crystals with microscopic photography. The discovery thoughts, both positive and negative, affect the water.

Take a look for yourself!

thank you!

you fool!

Think about it

What does this mean for you? More than half of our bodies are made up of water. If thoughts can impact water what else can they impact?

Another week went by and life in the hut got worse. The chickens clucked louder than before. The goat ran wild. The cow trampled everything. The poor man could hardly believe his misfortune. The man couldn't stand it. He ran to the Rabbi again, "It's a nightmare!" The Rabbi smiled and told the man to put all the animals back outside. The man thanked the Rabbi and ran back home.

That night the poor man and all his family slept peacefully. There was no crowing, no clucking and no honking. The next day the poor man ran back to the Rabbi. "Holy Rabbi," he cried, "You have made life sweet for me. With just my family in the hut, it's so peaceful. What a pleasure!"

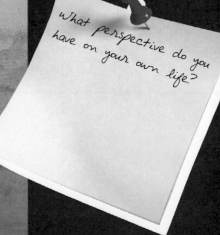

What perspective do you have on your own life?

9

Waves of Appreciation

If our thoughts are like boomerangs, why not use this to your advantage? Why not intentionally attract more good things in your life? Start a journal where you can reflect on and write about what is good in your life, more of it might show up! Some people call this a Gratitude Journal, call it what you like. We like to think of it as **Waves of Appreciation!** Here are a couple of ways you might ride the wave:

1. During the day, take 5 minutes to look around you and notice anything at all, however insignificant, that makes you feel good. It might be, "I'm having a great hair day", "That t-shirt looks cool on her", "I like how Paul treats his friends", "I don't feel angry right now", "I love how my dog is always happy to see me"... Have fun! You can either do this privately in your own mind (no one would even notice), or you can write in your journal.

2. Commit time each night or morning to write 3 things you appreciate or you're grateful for.

Over time, you might stop and think about how these simple forms of appreciation feel and how they affect your experience of happiness.

Tracking My Happiness

Track your happiness for one week. Too often we never even notice when we're happy! Stop and observe when you feel good. Use the space below to record: 1) Why did I feel happy? (e.g., time with friend, eating, new book), 2) What did I feel? (e.g., peacefulness, silliness, sore cheeks from laughing so hard), and 3) Rate your feeling of happiness using the scale below.

Rating Scale: 1 – 5
(i.e., 1 = calm and peaceful happy 5 = hyper crazy happy)

Date:	Why did I feel happy?	What did I feel?	Rating

What do you like better, the calm happy or the hyper happy?

Does Happiness Change?

"The art of living does not consist in preserving and clinging to a particular mode of happiness, but in allowing happiness to change its form without being disappointed by the change; happiness, like a child, must be allowed to grow up."

CHARLES L. MORGAN
British Novelist

Track what made you feel happy and **totally ALIVE** at different stages in your life using the timeline below (e.g., a pet, your favorite blanket, grandmother's hugs, family bonds, a relationship, etc.). Write, sketch...you decide.

Identify whether each item provided **short-term or long-term happiness.** What patterns do you notice between short and long-term happiness? What things have changed? What remains constant? Why?

Things that made me happy...

Infant   5 yrs.   10 yrs.

Our Journey

20 yrs.

25 yrs.

15 yrs.

I think that there is no exact definition for happiness, rather it's a feeling which makes us tension-free and joyful. What is more important for us to know is the reason behind why we feel happy. By nature, individuals have different ideologies. For example, a person who is very cruel might feel happy when he/she harms others or causes violence in society. Then, according to that person, this might be happiness, but for others it might be a pathetic situation. This can be confusing. So what I want to conclude here is what is needed for true happiness is a good heart.

YANGCHEN

Peter Block said something that really struck me. Besides living with freedom, he said that if someone ever tells you they lived their life without regret, they weren't paying enough attention. I strongly agree with this, because if you live your life in such a way that you think you'd do everything exactly the same, you obviously overlooked something. Everyone does stupid things in their life.

TOM

EXPLORING IN MY COMMUNITY

Interview one family or community member about how they see happiness. You might ask…

1. What makes you happy?

2. We've been exploring both short-term and long-term happiness. Can you share examples of both in your life?

3. Do you have any happiness tips?

Share your results with your family first, then your group or class. Using the results that each person brings from their interviews, create a large group mural, particularly two columns of short and long term happiness. What do you notice about any differences or similarities in the columns?

If you have web access, visit
www.projecthappiness.com
to see what others think about happiness!

My Six Happiness Tips

One person's view of happiness...Tal Ben-Shahar, author and lecturer at Harvard University, teaches the most popular course there called "Positive Psychology" to 1,400 students.

1. Give yourself permission to be human. When we accept emotions like fear, sadness, or anxiety as natural, we are more likely to overcome them. Rejecting our emotions, positive or negative, leads to frustration and unhappiness.

2. Happiness lies at the intersection between pleasure and meaning. Engage in activities that are both personally significant and enjoyable. If it's not possible, have happiness boosters, moments throughout the week that provide you with both pleasure and meaning.

3. Keep in mind that happiness is mostly dependent on our state of mind, not on our status or the state of our bank account. Barring extreme circumstances, our level of well being is determined by what we choose to focus on (the full or the empty part of the glass) and by our interpretation of external events. For example, do we view failure as catastrophic, or do we see it as a learning opportunity?

4. Simplify! We are, generally, too busy, trying to squeeze more and more activities into less and less time. Quantity influences quality, and we compromise on our happiness by trying to do too much.

5. Remember the mind-body connection. What we do or don't do with our bodies influences our mind. Regular exercise, adequate sleep, and healthy eating habits lead to both physical and mental health.

6. Express gratitude whenever possible. We too often take our lives for granted. Learn to appreciate and savor the wonderful things in life, from people to food, from nature to a smile.

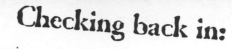

Checking back in:

→ What we all share in common: We all want more happiness and less pain in our lives.

→ What we don't share in common: One view of what happiness means.

→ There are 2 types of happiness: short-term and long-term. They both have their benefits & challenges.

→ Sometimes we get stuck in the "Never Ending Cycle of Desire" the more we get, the more we want.

→ The Boomerang Effect: The thoughts we put out into the world often come back into our lives.

→ Use the Boomerang Effect to your advantage, and start keeping a Gratitude Journal (Waves of Appreciation).

→ Thoughts are powerful, they even impact water so let's watch our thoughts with care.

What Do I NOW Know About Happiness?

How can I put this into action in my life?

II

OBSTACLES TO HAPPINESS

"History, despite its wrenching pain, cannot be unlived, but if faced with courage, need not be lived again."

-Maya Angelou

Acknowledging Pain

Just as we're all searching for happiness, we are also all trying to avoid or reduce pain in our lives. The reality is, however, that some pain and struggle are inescapable facts of a human life. We each experience difficulties in a variety of ways both large and small. Problems range from life's day-to-day small annoyances to the deep sorrow that comes from a life altering event. The degree and circumstance of our pain might vary from person to person and from culture to culture or even from one day to the next. We may even think that someone else's struggle is not so great, but in the mind and heart of the person it is very real. We also may think of pain as being mostly physical, like an injury or sickness, but often the more challenging issues that cause pain in our lives are those that aren't always visible, our inner struggles; things like self-doubt, depression, anxiety, anger. It is these types of emotional struggles that challenge our quest for happiness the most.

How do our struggles affect our quest for happiness?

Do we need them in some way to fully experience happiness?

Or is happiness found only in the absence of pain?

By starting with these questions we might begin to figure out how to best deal with struggle in our lives so we can find new paths to happiness.

ISOLATION

FEAR

ANXIETY

FAILURE

DEPRESSION

HURT

LOSS

ENVY

HOPELESSNESS

The Many Layers of Pain

ME

I feel invisible.
Who am I anyways?
What am I really here for?

GLOBALLY

I feel helpless!
- → Global warming
- → Tsunamis
- → Terrorism
- → Genocide
- → AIDS

What can **ONE** person do?

FRIENDS

I am a loner. No one cares.
All these dramas in my life it never ends!
Would anyone even miss me if I wasn't here?

FAMILY

I wish I had a family that cared about my needs.
No one in my family gets me.
I will never be who my parents want me to be.

COMMUNITY

What do they have to do with me?
I don't like their rules.
I'm not athletic and I'll never play in a band, so where do I fit in?
What do I have to offer?

Connected...Yet Disconnected

It is so easy these days to end up feeling alienated.
With technology we're more connected than ever; but also more physically and emotionally disconnected.

Two Faces

You see the outside, but what you really don't know about me is...

Online Socializing

I'm spending so much time here, but is anyone REALLY listening?

Music

Music makes me feel alive, but what happens when the song ends? I still feel the same.

My Story

What kind of difficulties do you face in your own life on personal, family, community, and global levels?

How connected do you feel to those around you?

Express what is real for you. Write it. Sketch it.

The REALITY Is...

Struggle is a part of life.

The GOOD NEWS Is...

You have a choice of how you respond...the power is within YOU!

Man's Search for Meaning
BY VICKTOR FRANKL

Even in incredibly inhumane and horrific situations there is always some potential for self-realization and unbelievable good. That thought always surprises me, no matter how many times I hear it. Viktor Frankl was a Nazi death camp survivor, yet after this horror, Frankl was not a broken man of lost faith. He somehow realized a new human potential in the midst of such despair. He makes me consider the possibility that even in the most devastating conditions, there is a great opportunity for the human spirit. In his book, *Man's Search for Meaning*, he brings forth the notion that even though we cannot choose our circumstances, as conscious humans we have the ultimate power to decide our reactions to those circumstances. Granted, it takes a remarkable person to realize this when staring hopelessness in the face, but the thought that it is possible can give hope and sustain one's faith in humanity. In reading his story I saw that even in the bleakest circumstances, with the right response, we can still find our humanity and ultimately happiness.

AARON
Student, USA

HAPPINESS TOOLS

How do we do THAT?? Here are some tools. Use one or all, it's up to you.

"Our attitude towards suffering changes how we experience it."
-EMILY

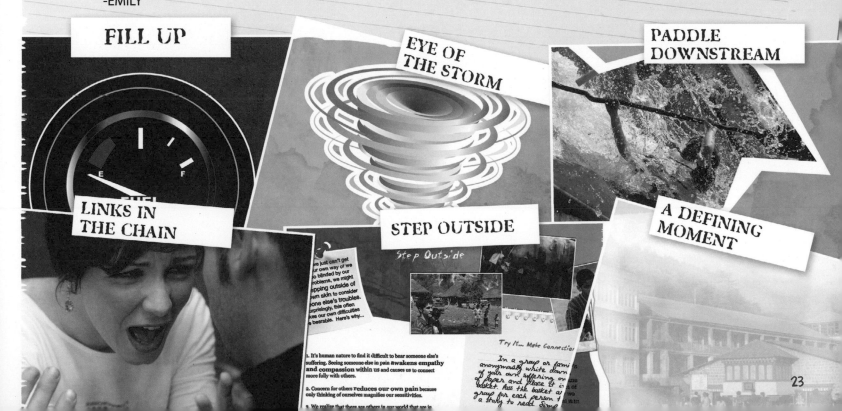

FILL UP

EYE OF THE STORM

PADDLE DOWNSTREAM

LINKS IN THE CHAIN

STEP OUTSIDE

Step Outside

A DEFINING MOMENT

...e just can't get ...ur own way or we ...o blinded by our ...roblems, we might ...pping outside of ...wn skin to consider ...one else's troubles. ...urprisingly, this often ...kes our own difficulties ...bearable. Here's why...

1. It's human nature to find it difficult to bear someone else's suffering. Seeing someone else in pain **awakens empathy and compassion** within us and causes us to connect more fully with others.

2. Concern for others **reduces our own pain** because only thinking of ourselves magnifies our sensitivities.

3. We realize that there are others in our world that are in...

Try It... Make Connection

In a group or famil... anonymously write down... of your own suffering on one of paper and place it in a of basket. Pass the basket a... group for each person t... a story to read. Som...

Fill Up!

Two very common reactions when we're faced with struggle in our lives are "what did I do to deserve this?" and "I guess this is what I deserve." Yes, we need to take responsibility for our actions, but there is a difference between being responsible and creating stories that are counterproductive to our happiness. Perhaps we might look at struggle in a new way...as a

warning sign, like an empty gas gauge.

It is NOT an sign of who you are or your worthiness, but rather it's a sign that can help you...
MAKE A CHOICE!

A. Okay, I should fill up. How?... by thinking or doing something better.

B. Great, now I'll never make it to my destination. Yeah, life sucks.

Just like we'd fill up our cars with gas if they indicated empty, struggle in our lives is a sign for us to fill ourselves up.

We can experience pain and turn our thoughts to what we **DO** want in our lives. Remember our thoughts are like boomerangs. Change our thoughts = change our experience.
OR
We can experience pain and fear and dwell in the suffering.

We can make a choice now or wait until we get an even **BIGGER** warning sign later. It is up to us!

Reflecting on Struggle...Write, sketch, rap.

Think of a struggle you have faced in your life either recently or in the past. What warning signs (big or small) have shown up in relation to this struggle? How have you responded to them?

The thing that destroys my happiness is an abrupt change that ends in the loss of a friendship. Friends and family are the most important things to me, and when my friends either leave or something comes between us, it saddens me greatly. I think that friends are the most critical things to being happy.
TOM

I agree with Tom; I find happiness through my relationships with others, and likewise that happiness is destroyed when those relationships end. Nothing makes me more happy than laughing and playing with my friends and family, the people I love. And nothing makes me more sad than the loss of that love. So interestingly enough, my happiness and sadness are completely dependent on the same things.
JONJI

What makes me unhappy, or destroys my happiness, is like what John said, when a good friend, or anyone around me, is unhappy. Their unhappiness pulls me down too. I am easily affected by other people's moods. Besides that, I think hearing about all the bad things that are happening in the world destroys my happiness.
JEREMY

The Eye of the Storm

Probably the scariest thing about being human is living in a world with things over which we seem to have no power – sickness, natural disasters, the end of life. Even day-to-day struggles can be intense and sometimes outside of our own control, like other people's choices and attitudes. Although we can't always control the outside, we DO have some control over the inside: HOW we respond to our circumstances. The degree to which pain and struggle affect us is up to us.

Life can seem like a tornado – it's unpredictable and turbulent, but we can still find a place of stillness in the center of the storm. Even if everyone and everything around us is caught up in the chaos, we can choose where we want to hang out.

Choose to get swept up into the twister and have our emotions escalate out of control, OR find a calm center in the eye of the storm.

"I have no real friends."

"My friend ignored me."

"I'm such a liar!"

Excuses for my teacher:

"Late for school"

"Woke up late!"

Eye of the Storm:
"Hey, I'm human."
"She must be having a bad day –
I'll give her a call later."

Where I Choose to Hang out: Write, sketch, or Rap.

Where do I usually find myself in the twister or whirlwind? What do I normally say to myself in this place during a struggle? How has this location affected the way in which I deal with struggle in my life? What can I do to move closer to the Eye of the Storm?

Paddle Downstream
Equipment Required: INNER GUIDANCE SYSTEM

Throughout our lives we are faced with contrasting experiences (i.e., ones we **DO** want and those we **DON'T** want). Within each of us is an **INNER GUIDANCE SYSTEM** constantly telling us how each of these experiences feels (i.e., good or bad). When it feels good at the core, we are aligned with our true nature. When some part of us feels bad, we're off course. Although our **INNER GUIDANCE SYSTEM** is **VERY** reliable, sometimes we don't take the time to listen and trust it. First we need to be open to hearing it. Then we can choose how we respond to this innate wisdom within us.

How we respond can be compared to paddling a boat **upstream** or **downstream**.

Paddle Upstream - NO!

Paddle downstream - YES!

Against the current.

Going with the Flow!

Feels **BAD!**
Not fun, constant struggle, anxiety, not myself.

Feels **GOOD!**
Energized, happy, peaceful, feels right.

TURN YOUR BOAT AROUND
When something feels **BAD**, turn your boat around by thinking of what you **DO** want in your life. Do what feels **GOOD**, what feels **RIGHT**.

Which Direction Do I Choose to Paddle?

What struggles do you NOT want in your life? How can you turn your boat around and rephrase your thoughts into what you DO want?

DON'T WANT IN MY LIFE:
(What thoughts wear me down?)

There is so much drama in my life!

This assignment is totally stressing me out!

DO WANT IN MY LIFE:
(What thoughts empower me?)

I can now see the drama in my life and how I get sucked into it. I can take a step back and choose not to get wrapped up in it.

I know I'll get through this. I always do. I'll just work on this small part for now and get help with the rest. One step at a time.

The Links in the Chain

The Dalai Lama says that "there is often a gap between the way in which we perceive events and the reality of a given situation; it is the source of much unhappiness."

All too often we take an isolated event or situation and label it as the truth of who we are or what our life is meant to be. We don't relate it to the many events or circumstances surrounding it. In this way, we are only seeing a very small piece of the puzzle. When we take a step back to observe the chain of events that led to our current situation, we might realize...

Everything is connected to something that happened before.

CONFLICT!!

Nothing else matters.

If something happens to her how will I go on?

My mom was just diagnosed with cancer.

I just want to curl up in a ball in the corner by myself.

I can't sleep or eat.

My best friend just shut me out of her life.

Reflecting on Cause and Effect

Can you think of a recent struggle you experienced in your life where you didn't consider the various factors that could have led to it?

If you try to consider these other variables, does it change your view of the situation? If so, how?

OK guys, get ready, this one is a toughie: Why do people try to avoid conflict so much? Can someone be losing out on happiness because they are trying so hard to avoid inevitable quarrels? I think that for people to grow mentally they have to deal with the ups and downs of relationships.
NINA

We need to be more informed about the nature of life and duality of our existence (i.e. without sorrow there is no happiness, no pain-no gain, no sweat-no sweet etc.)
DORJI

Step Outside

When we just can't get out of our own way or we are too blinded by our own problems, we might try stepping outside of our own skin to consider someone else's troubles. Surprisingly, this often makes our own difficulties more bearable. Here's why...

1. It's human nature to find it difficult to bear someone else's suffering. Seeing someone else in pain **awakens empathy and compassion within us** and causes us to connect more fully with others.

2. Concern for others **reduces our own pain** because only thinking of ourselves magnifies our sensitivities.

3. We realize that there are others in our world that are in **much worse condition than we are.**

4. We notice that **we ALL have the power** to not only withstand difficulties, **but to discover the depth of our inner strength,** courage, and kindness toward others.

Try It! Make Connections:

In a group or family, anonymously write down a story of your own suffering on a piece of paper and place it in a group basket. Pass the basket around the group for each person to pick out a story to read. Simply listen.

If you are alone, interview friends and family you are comfortable with. Ask them about past challenges they might have faced and how they dealt with them.

Reflecting on Others' Suffering

What observations did you make about the connection between our awareness of others and their struggles and our own pain?

Have any of your past difficulties helped you feel more connected to others or feel more empathy for them? If so, how?

The one thing that really got me was meeting with the kids at the Tibetan Children's Village, because they are basically orphans. They didn't have parents with them and they didn't complain, they just told their stories with a smile on their faces. For me, that was really touching, because I'm an orphan too and it's really hard to connect with people. I have a really hard time telling people I'm an orphan and I'm sad about it. Just knowing that they are orphans and have so much happiness and confidence in who they are…it really changed me.
PRABHA

My moment was when we were at the Kingsway Camp and we were with the children. It was just so beautiful to hear their prayer because they're considered the lowest of the low in the caste system, the untouchables, but when they sang their voices were just so vibrant and loud and beautiful. They've been dealt a bad hand in life but nothing was going to silence them, they were still going to sing loudly and give praise. It was just really beautiful to hear that.
NINA

Our Journey

The Dalai Lama speaks a lot about the importance of suffering in one's life. Indeed, so much of what is inspiring about the Dalai Lama, is a product of his suffering and of the suffering of his people. The fact that his people suffer has given him a purpose in life: to try to find an end to their exile, both internal and external.

As we discuss this in class, it becomes apparent that all the people that we admire in history have been driven to action because of an inner discontent with the state of the world or the state of their people. When you look at our heroes, people like Nelson Mandela, Mahatma Gandhi, and Martin Luther King, it becomes apparent that they have all experienced extreme persecution. Perhaps in order to achieve great things, we must experience some suffering.
DANIEL

From the moment we are born, there is sadness. Tibetans say that children cry because they leave their mother's womb, which is so smooth that even silk is rough to their skin. So we come into this world with the known fact of sadness from birth. So that's why we know what happiness is, as we feel it in our soul.
YONTEN

A Defining Moment

We can also look outside of ourselves to others who have not only suffered, but who have overcome great suffering with dignity and determination. For the people we admire the most, suffering was a defining moment because they were able to figure out who they really were and all they were capable of being, even in the darkest of times. We too have this opportunity.

Today was our first day visiting Tibetan Children's Village (TCV).

At dinner one of the Tibetan students sat next to me, his name was Ngawang. As we ate, he told me his story: "I lived in a small village in Tibet with my family until I was about 11 years old. Me and the other village children didn't know we were under Chinese rule."

I asked him how he had come to live at TCV.

"One day my father told me that we were going to cross the border into Nepal, a 3 or 4 day walk. We could only travel at night; we slept during the day.

"Right before the border there was a very fast and dangerous river. Two people from my group lost their lives. After we made it across, the Nepali people at the border asked us Tibetans for money. If we did not give them enough money, they would turn us into the Chinese who paid them. We reached a check-post and we got enough money together to get past the Nepali guards.

"My father and I walked to the bus station and took a bus to my Auntie who lived in Nepal. From there she sent me to TCV. I have not seen my father since I left Nepal; he went back to Tibet to care for my mother. Recently, he wrote me that he has until June of this year to demolish his house and rebuild it in the Chinese style."

The magnitude of the story and Ngawang's openness in telling it left me in awe. He did not seem sad at any point; in fact, quite the opposite. "How is it now, being so far away from home?" I asked, emboldened by his openness.

"When I first reached TCV, many nights I cried in my bed, as did many others. It is sad to be so far away, but I know I am here for the better. Back in my village, there is very poor medicine; people lose their lives from simple things that can easily be cured. I'm going to become a physician. I am going to learn how to help all my friends and family back home."

As a group, discuss people you know who have found an opportunity in times of great challenge in their lives and defined themselves as a result.

My Defining Moments...

Our own story does not have to be on the epic scale of the Dalai Lama or other legendary figures, but perhaps we too can look at struggle as an opportunity.

How have I defined myself in my response to my own struggles?

If I look closely enough, can I find any opportunities in my past struggles?

In class we talked about finding the opportunity in suffering. Here are a couple of our stories:

SUFFERING:
Father being really sick.

OPPORTUNITY:
• You get to spend time with him.
• Perhaps if one of your friends has a sick parent, you can empathize (you will have compassion).
• Appreciation for who he is and how important he is in your life.

SUFFERING:
I didn't get into my top picks for colleges.

OPPORTUNITY:
• I realize that there are teens all over the world that will never have a chance to go to college.
• I'm grateful I CAN go to college.
• I might end up at the perfect college for me and it will change my future.

Bunthoeun

Trying to Prove Myself

From what I can remember, growing up has always been a challenge because I feel like I have to prove myself to others. As the oldest son of a family from a poor background with little knowledge of America, I knew that I had a lot of growing up to do, and a lot of proving mainly to myself.

My first of many challenges started in childhood with my friends at school. We would play hopscotch, four squares, high jump, marbles, and a variety of other games. I was always teased and picked last on teams, as the weakest player. I was frail. Not being recognized as equal or accepted made me angry, frustrated, and lonely. I thought for a period of time that I was wrong for being me. I wanted to change who I was, so I started fights at school just to prove that I was tough enough to be recognized by my peers. I got into a lot of trouble, was suspended, and had many parent-teacher conferences.

Finding a Release

After a while I couldn't stand the punishment and was afraid of disappointing my parents. So I picked up a pencil and paper and began writing. I learned how to cope with my rage and frustration by venting on paper. It's hard to explain, but I was just able to relax.

It was a crazy emotional state I went through. I was in a deep trench, a mental state of being a "nobody" so that I became angry with myself at times for no reason. I wanted to be stronger, bigger, and faster. But I didn't know how. I had to find a way to make myself become what I wanted, so I turned to my interest in art. I was looking for a way to escape the harsh reality of my life and I made it possible with my art.

→ That REALITY is struggle is a part of life.

→ The GOOD NEWS is you have a choice in how you respond. The power is within YOU!

   o We can Fill Ourselves Up with what we DO want in our life.

   o We can try to find the calm place in the Eye of the Storm, when everything around us is chaos!

   o We can Paddle Downstream by doing what feels good at the core.

   o We can open our eyes to the Links in the Chain - the many events that led to our struggle.

   o We can Step Outside ourselves and consider someone elsé pain, rather than just our own.

   o We can look for opportunities in our struggles, our Defining Moments.

What Do I NOW Know about Happiness?

How can I put this into action in my life?

III

SELF-REFLECTION

"Know thyself."

— Socrates

Do Any of These Appeal to You?

O I'd like to figure out why I do the things I do.
O I'd like to say that I really know who I am.
O I'd like to have some control over my thoughts and feelings.
O I'd like to feel calm more often than not.
O I'd like to be able to make better decisions and not just react to things around me.
O I'd like to feel good about the choices I make.
O I'd like to feel happy about myself.

Are you willing to take the first step?

Choices that Bring Happiness

More Empowering Thoughts & Feelings

Self-Awareness

Self-Reflections

Actions

Thoughts & Feeling

So why bother?

All of these are possible when we take the time to get to know ourselves, how we think, feel, and act (or react). One step at a time, with emotional honesty, we can get to know who we are and what we are fully capable of. With that comes an opportunity to own our lives and make choices that empower us and bring about happiness. It takes courage to take the first step, but the ascent is worth it.

Who Am I?

What Others See...
Write or sketch how you think others see you.

How I See Myself...
What they don't know about me is...

The Boomerang Effect

Is there a connection between what others see in me and what I focus on in myself? How do I want people to know me? What thoughts can I focus on so others know me that way?

Wave of Appreciation

In your journal, write 3 things about yourself that you are proud of or happy for.

Try this for a week

What's Getting Your Wheels Spinning?

How we THINK, FEEL, & ACT (OR REACT) whether we realize it or not, work like gears. One cannot function without impacting the other, because they are all tightly connected to one another. Sometimes our thoughts spark an emotion, other times a feeling might get our mind spinning, and yes, even a choice in how we act might engage our emotional roller coaster.

When we REACT to an external circumstance, we are blindly letting the situation outside of us influence our response. When we ACT, we intentionally choose how we'll respond to the situation.

Let's take a closer look at how thoughts, feelings, or actions can get our wheels spinning and dictate our lives.

My Wheels in Motion

Observe your thoughts, feelings, and actions for one day this week. Record what you observe. Did a thought initiate a feeling or did your feelings influence your actions? When you recognize a connection, place an arrow in that direction (T to F to A).

If you had a chance to rewrite these scenes, what would they look like?

Who's Flyin' the Plane?

What is a thought? Not being aware of the thoughts that arise in our mind allows them to dominate our lives. Unnoticed, they have great power. Sometimes our thoughts run on autopilot and we're not even aware of them. Other times we are aware of what we're thinking, so we are intentional with our thoughts. We can start observing the power of words in our life by taking time to objectively notice our thoughts. With new awareness and time, we can start expanding our helpful thought patterns and break our addiction to the unhelpful ones.

Intentional!
(We're at the controls)

HELPFUL: for choosing what you want and how you want to live. You're in the driver's seat! You intentionally choose thoughts that bring you more happiness rather than less.

NOT SO HELPFUL: Sometimes it takes more time and work to turn off the negative autopilot thoughts and come up with empowering ones.
"This is challenging, but I always find a way."
"Sometimes I learn the most about my strength in tougher situations."
"I might not be great at math, but I can rhyme like nobody's business."

Autopilot!
(Who's flyin' the plane?)

HELPFUL: for riding a bike, remembering directions to school, eating, or surviving sudden danger. Why? It saves us time and energy because we don't have to think and plan. It just happens.

NOT SO HELPFUL: Negative self-talk:
"I'll NEVER get it!"
"Why Is life always so tough?"
"It's true, I'm stupid."

Ask Yourself: Which of these thoughts get me what I want?

What kind of story are you seeing on the screen? Look deeply into the script. What are your plans for the protagonist? What thoughts, helpful and unhelpful, are shaping your story? Are you happy with your script or are you considering a rewrite? You choose.

Imagine you are the writer, director and actor in your own movie.

Who's Playing in My Jungle?

Have you been feeding your Monkey Mind? What have you noticed about the tapes you play in your mind? Do you tend to catastrophize, blame, or personalize the events in your life. Are these thoughts empowering or defeating? Where do you think these messages come from (your own misinterpretations, your friends, family, the music you listen to, the media you watch)? Write, sketch...

Waves of Appreciation

Talk to someone you feel comfortable with about these new observations. Ask them to simply listen. You might then invite them to share their perspective. Express your appreciation for this person in your Gratitude Journal.

Changing Our Mindset

Carol Dweck, world-renowned Stanford University psychologist, talks about the power of our mindset or our beliefs (especially around challenge). We can either have a Fixed Mindset where we let failure (or even success) define who we are, or a Growth Mindset where we see setbacks as opportunities to grow and improve ourselves. Just like how we learned to walk. There are many stumbles along the way, but to reach our potential and live the life we desire, it takes practice and perseverance. We always have a choice about which view we adopt for ourselves. It's never too late to change. What's your view?

It's up to you!

FIXED MINDSET
Belief that my intelligence, personality, and character are carved in stone; my potential is determined at birth.

GROWTH MINDSET
Belief that my intelligence, personality, and character can be developed. A person's true potential is unknown (and unknowable).

	FIXED MINDSET	GROWTH MINDSET
DESIRE	Look smart in every situation and prove myself over and over again. Never fail!!	Stretch myself, take risks and learn. Bring on the challenges!
EVALUATION OF SITUATIONS	Will I succeed or fail? Will I look smart or dumb?	Will this allow me to grow? Will this help me overcome some of my challenges?
DEALING WITH SETBACKS	"I'm a failure." (identity) "I'm an idiot."	"I failed." (action) "I'll try harder next time."
CHALLENGES	Avoid challenges, get defensive or give up easily.	Embrace challenges, persist in the face of setbacks.
EFFORT	Why bother? It's not going to change anything.	Growth and learning require effort.
CRITICISM	Ignore constructive criticism.	Learn from criticism. How can I improve?
SUCCESS OF OTHERS	Feel threatened by the success of others. If you succeed, then I fail.	Finds lessons & inspiration in other people's success.
RESULT...	Plateau early, achieve less than my full potential.	Reach ever-higher levels of achievement.

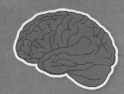

Reflecting on My Mindset

What kind of mindset do you currently hold for yourself? How does it impact your life? Was there a time in your life that you held a growth mindset? What did it feel like? What steps can you take to open up to a growth mindset?

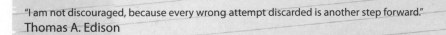

"I am not discouraged, because every wrong attempt discarded is another step forward."
Thomas A. Edison

Did you know...

Thomas Edison tried more than 9,000 experiments before he successfully invented the first light bulb.

Bill Gates, founder of Microsoft & the richest man in the world for the last decade, is a Harvard University dropout.

Ludwig von Beethoven, one of the world's most famous composers, was deaf.

Michael Jordan, one of the greatest basketball players of all time, was cut from his high school basketball team because of his "lack of skill".

Walt Disney's first cartoon production company went bankrupt.

Our Journey

Why did you get into neuro-science?

From very early on, I had the conviction that the mind is something that is very important to our well-being and happiness. If we can all improve our mind in certain ways, then we can improve our well-being and the world would be a better place.

In science, it was clear that if I wanted to study the mind, I had to study the brain, so I got involved in brain research. Neuroplasticity is a relatively new discovery in the last 10 – 15 years. When I was in graduate school we were taught that we were born with a fixed number of brain cells. We now know that's totally wrong. We now know that the average adult grows 5,000 new brain cells a day. They're critical for new learning and memory. We can now understand how training our mind can actually produce enduring changes. This is terrifically exciting!
Richard Davidson
world-renowned neuroscientist

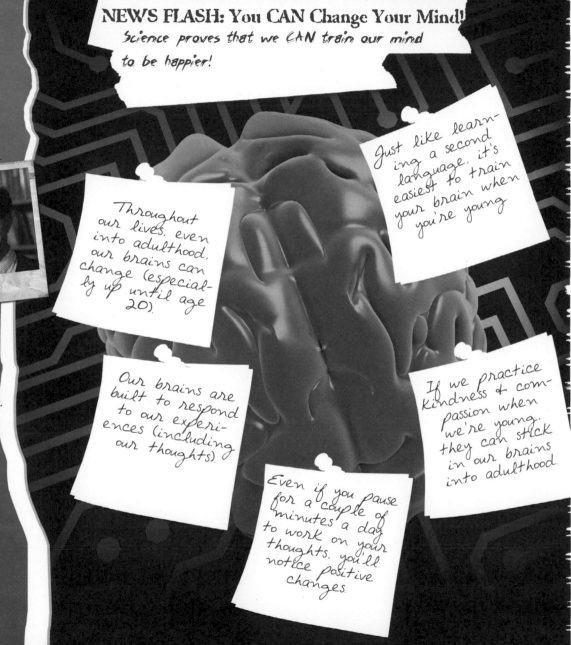

NEWS FLASH: You CAN Change Your Mind!
Science proves that we CAN train our mind to be happier!

Just like learning a second language, it's easiest to train your brain when you're young.

Throughout our lives, even into adulthood, our brains can change (especially up until age 20).

Our brains are built to respond to our experiences (including our thoughts).

If we practice kindness + compassion when we're young, they can stick in our brains into adulthood.

Even if you pause for a couple of minutes a day to work on your thoughts, you'll notice positive changes.

52

Training My Brain

If you play a sport or a musical instrument, you know what we mean by training. You know the daily regimen or schedule you commit to, to master your craft. Even learning a new language or taking a new course require a "practice". Well, training your brain to develop new skills is no different. It's just a matter of finding a practice that allows you to work on your thoughts in a way that suits your personality and interests. It might be 10 minutes of meditation each day, a couple of minutes in bed each night listening to soothing music, a run in the park, or a weekly conversation with friends. What thoughts would you like to improve? Set some goals and find a practice that is meaningful to you. You might not see changes over night; it's a gradual process, but it IS possible to change your brain!

What kinds of new "mind" skills do you want to develop (love, courage, gratitude, patience, confidence)? What would your training "practice" look like (what would you say to yourself: where and when would you say it)?

Try It!
Set a goal, find a practice, and try it for a week. What do you notice? Share your findings with friends, family, or your class.

Floating in Isolation

Just like we can go through our lives feeding our Monkey Minds or viewing the world with a Fixed Mindset, many of us fall into the trap of either denying or attaching to our emotions. Many of us have been socialized to put on a brave face at all cost! Sometimes we "suck it up" to maintain our tough front, other times we get latched onto a random thought and yet other times we just shut down emotionally to avoid being hurt. Often our pain runs very deep. Like an iceberg, we often only see the tip of our emotions, with the rest concealed deep inside, hidden from others and even from ourselves. Understandably, we're all just trying to cope with life and its inevitable struggles, but when we deny ourselves emotions we become frigid and frozen also like an iceberg. We also become more vulnerable. We know that one little tear drop, conflict or moment of weakness will either melt our cold front (which we've been holding in for years) or crack us into pieces. We live in constant fear of breaking down!

If only we could have some compassion for ourselves and the range of feelings we ALL will encounter in the human experience. With a little warmth, we might melt away some of our rigidity and feel a new sense of flow with ourselves and those around us.

We're all made of water after all, so everyone has the capacity to freeze up or flow together.

Surfacing Emotions

Do you push your emotions to the surface?

Are there certain situations that are harder to keep in the light, where you feel the urge to push them under the surface?

What steps could you take to bring them up to the surface?

How could you have compassion toward yourself when the emotions that you hoped to hide come to the surface?

Our Journey

Yangchen spoke of a very important idea; that sometimes these feelings happen all on their own, without any reason. What I wanted to add is that it is interesting how many of our feelings and emotions come from an inward place. Often our feelings of happiness or sadness do not come from an obvious place. Sometimes the feeling comes from deep within us, where we might have a hard time locating it.
JOHN NURI

I was just thinking about the project, and I came to the conclusion that if we are to find out what makes us truly happy, we must also find out what makes us sad.
JONJI

Uncovering the Mystery of Emotions

Although emotions are mysterious to many of us, without them we would truly be LOST. They are our INNER GUIDANCE SYSTEM—like a compass, they give us essential information about which direction to head. Distressing or negative emotions signal that we are Paddling Upstream. Although these emotions might not feel good (we feel like we are Paddling against the current), they do help us. They are telling us we don't like something and we might want to change direction. Anger might help us stand up for our values, while fear might save us from danger. It's when we get stuck in these emotions that they can be destructive. Emotions that feel good, meanwhile, signal that we are Paddling Downstream so we might want to keep going with the flow. All emotions, distressing or pleasant, exist to help us. We need to pay closer attention so we know when and where to turn our boat around. It might help to better understand where these emotions come from:

FACT: Emotions are physical.

1. An action or a thought can trigger an emotion that comes to life in the form of a biochemical that goes to every cell in your body.

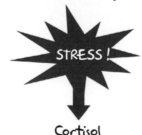

STRESS !

Cortisol

IN LOVE

Dopamine
Epinephrine
Phenylethylamine

2. These biochemicals only last 6 seconds, unless they trigger our thoughts, which then make them last longer. We build them into something bigger (a.k.a Monkey Mind)!

It's like a cascade effect. The more we think of them, the more biochemicals are released, and the stronger the feeling! Then they really get into motion, becoming intense "e-motions."

Mastering Our Emotions

When we do get to that place where we feel **stuck in our negative or distressing emotions** (anxiety, fear, anger, disappointment, etc.), frantically Paddling Upstream out of control. There are tricks we can use to **turn our boat around.** Now that we know that our negative emotions exist to inform us, and that they might only last **a few seconds**, we can choose to stop their flow once we get the information we need. Anger doesn't need to develop into rage, fear doesn't need to lead into panic, and disappointment doesn't need to grow into hopelessness. We might speak our truth, walk away, journal, ACT instead of REACT, or try one of these quick, but powerful tricks that **use our minds to calm our bodies!** When our feelings have hijacked our mind, we're triggered or ready to explode, let's try one of these:

Get Grounded!

Close your eyes and imagine that you have tree roots or a cord coming out of the bottom of your feet, connecting you to the ground. It might also be a garbage shoot. Whatever it looks like, imagine that with every exhale, you're dumping your stress into the earth to dissolve. With every inhale, imagine feeling lighter and lighter.

Let Go!

Find a place to sit, feel your feet on the ground, your back against the floor/chair. Notice the air coming in through your nose and mouth and filling your lungs. As you inhale, think of the word "let" and as you exhale imagine the word "go". Keep it going try to get into a rhythm!

The 5 Second PAUSE button

→ Sing 5 lines of your favorite song.
→ Remember 5 of your friends' names.
→ Think of 5 things you love to do.

Warm Up

Once you've released the distressing stuff, fill yourself up with the good stuff. Imagine a golden sun at the top of your head. Fill it with all of the things that feel great (courage, strength, love, kindness, hope). Then follow the sun down through your heart and torso, feeling it warm up every part of your body. Relax and feel the warmth.

5 Breaths!

1. Breathe in (calm) for 5 seconds.
2. Then hold your breath for 5 seconds.
3. Then breathe out (stress) for 5 seconds.
4. Repeat steps 1 - 3 until you feel relief.

57

Mental Test Drive

Just like you'd test drive a car before making the big purchase, let's test drive these mental techniques to see which one might be worth putting into action in your own life on a regular basis. There isn't one car that suits everyone's needs, nor is there one calming method that suits each and every one of us. Try one the 5 methods mentioned before, perhaps one for a day or two, and then write any observations below. How did it feel? Were you comfortable doing this? How did it affect your emotions: better, worse, neutral? How did it affect your response to the situation?

You might also come up with your own calming technique or ask around to see what others do to handle their emotions and test drive those techniques too. It's all about finding the right match!!

Method	Observations
<u>Example:</u> The 5 Second Pause Button.	In the middle of a fight with my girlfriend, I starting thinking of the lyrics to my favorite song. By just escaping for a few seconds, I felt like I turned the "crazy" switch off and was able to think more clearly. I was then able to hear her side of the story more easily. The neat thing is that no one needs to know what I'm thinking...not even her.

Bunthoeun's Story

Art Lets Me Choose

For hours I would create an imaginary storyline filled with characters I could play. I would draw for hours until I was satisfied. It also helped keep me out of trouble. I am not the best artist in the world, but I control the way the characters look, I decide the clothes the wear. Will they be good or bad? this makes me happy. It's my choice. Drawing taught me patience, peace, and tranquility. I knew then that I found my alternate way to deal with my rage, frustration, and anger.

I had a few more turning points in my life; I was in a middle school gang, jumping members in, and skipping most of my classes. Soon I realized I didn't want to live that lifestyle for long. Plus, one of the gang members burglarized my home. I was ready to bring my own justice if I found out who did it.

I didn't find out who it was until a few years later-after I had quit my gang lifestyle of violence and revenge. I chose to forgive him and forgive myself. A sigh of relief flowed from my breath that day when I made the choice to move on.

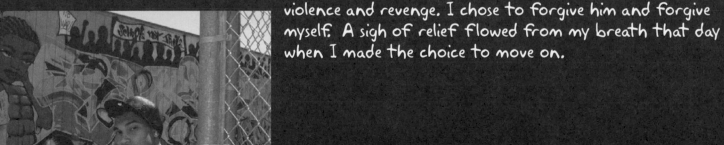

Emotions Study

Have you felt any of these emotions this past week? Circle at least 3 of those you experienced. In your journal, write about what these feelings felt like physically and emotionally (E.g. stressed, tight chest, back ache, can't focus, uncomfortable, think the worst, feel horrible all over). Describe each one enough so you might be able to better recognize it earlier next time. Try the whole list if you like.

Try It...
Share this page with your friends or your family, then talk about the experience together.

Angry	Sad	Happy	Proud
Confident	Annoyed	Embarrassed	Compassionate
Serious	Shy	Hopeful	Disappointed
Frustrated	Silly	Guilty	Scared
Anxious	Depressed	Resentful	Loving
Brave	Capable	Careless	Excited
Jealous	Stressed	Hopeless	Inspired

Your emotions are here to guide you! What does Paddling Upstream or Downstream feel like? Track your emotions for a day or two. See if you are able to identify the actual emotion you are feeling at different points during the day. It's not always easy. fear and stress might feel the same for example. Then identify the feeling as a positive feeling (Downstream with the flow) or negative feeling (Upstream against the current). Describe each feeling both physically and emotionally. what have you learned about your Inner Guidance System? Look at the patterns in both columns.

Paddling Upstream
(negative feelings)

Paddling Downstream
(positive feelings)

What thoughts might help you move from paddling frantically upstream to flowing effortlessly downstream with the natural current?

The Guest House

This being human is a guest house. Every morning a new arrival. A joy, a depression, a meanness, some momentary awareness comes as an unexpected visitor.
Welcome and entertain them all!
Even if they're a crowd of sorrows who violently sweep your house empty of its furniture, still treat each guest honorably.
He may be clearing you out for some new delight.
The dark thought, the shame, the malice, meet them at the door laughing, and invite them in.
Be grateful for whoever comes, because each has been sent as a guide from beyond.

RUMI

Try It...

If we treat our emotions as friends, new or old, we might treat them more objectively and with some compassion. Invite them into your home, but only feed the ones you want to stay for a while. Imagine the conversation you might have with them:

Think About It...

What would you say to your feelings if they were a guest? What would be real for you?

Hey Anger...you're steaming! What's going on?

Love, what took you so long? I've got a spot for you right here!

Sadness, what's up? Grab a seat, tell me more.

Fear...my long lost friend, don't worry, we always make it through.

Tracking the Four Rivers

We can also learn more about ourselves by looking at our responses to what Angeles Arrien, cultural anthropologist, author, and educator calls the Four Rivers. She shares that there are four rivers in each of our experiences: Inspiration, Surprise, Challenge, and Love. Through self-reflection we can learn more about how we paddle down these rivers at different points each day.

River of INSPIRATION:
The River of Inspiration lights the creative fire, which is known by indigenous cultures as the fire that does not need wood.

Who or what inspired me today? What is inspiring me in a team? Who or what is inspiring me in the community?

River of SURPRISE:
The River of Surprise is about flexibility and resilience in response to whatever may come our way. The Inuit people say that there are two plans to every day: my plan and mysterys' plan. Surprise shows us where we are still flexible or not flexible.

How did I handle surprise today? How did I handle changes in my plans? How much of my happiness is dependent on routine?

River of CHALLENGE:
The River of Challenge is an invitation to grow and to stretch, to reach beyond the knowable, to observe when we feel challenged and let it be a source of strength. Accepting challenge allows our creative muscle to be developed.

Who or what challenged me today? How many possibilities and perspectives can I handle? In places of ambiguity, how tolerant am I and resistant to the chaos?

River of LOVE:
The River of Love is simply an examination of the things that have great meaning in our lives, which can give you a strong sense of gratitude and connection to others.

What am I learning about love? What has touched or moved me? For what or who am I grateful?

63

Our Journey

Yesterday, Angeles Arrien came into the classroom with a purpose. This was a little bit unfamiliar for me. Most of our guests come with the intention of answering our questions. Angeles knew that she had something valuable to share with us and that was exciting for me, because it seemed like she'd put a lot of thought into what kind of practice she could share with us that would really help us.

On Wednesday, she decided to talk to us about tracking our experiences using the four rivers as a structure. The four rivers are inspiration, love, surprise and challenge. The method that Angeles suggested was that each day, at the end of our day, we look back upon our day and ask ourselves what inspired us, what surprised us, what challenged us and where we experienced love. I believe that this will prove a valuable method for me if I should choose to employ it, which I hope to. If someone who's lived and experienced and taught as much as Angeles, believes so strongly in regular self-reflection, then there must be some truth to it.
-DANIEL

Tracking My Four Rivers

What inspired me today?

What challenged me today?

What surprised me today?

What touched my heart or made me feel grateful today?

Waves of Appreciation

Try this exercise daily in your journal for a week as a form of appreciation

The Gift

When we recognize what **inspires us**, makes us **feel totally alive or grateful**, we are tapping into our true nature, the **pure goodness within us.** This is what we need to trust in figuring out who we really are. Sobonfu Some, teacher of indigenous wisdom, elaborates on this idea in the African story **the Gift.**

Every person born into a family brings a special gift that the community needs. It is the job of the elders to make sure the child's gift is realized. Instead of merely seeing children as blank slates from birth who are then filled with education and ideas of right and wrong, adults can benefit and learn from the child's gift. As a young person, in order to realize your gift you must come from a place of strength. Sobonfu Some says, "Make a list of all the things that make you strong. Even if it's hard for you to bring each one out every day, just say 'I am great, because I can make people laugh.'" Pick a gift that you think reflects you. Then the most important thing for the community to do is to help you build confidence about your gift through positive reinforcement. Without confidence in your gift, whatever it may be, you won't be able to help yourself or anyone else. You need to have courage and stay true to who you are on the inside to help your gift emerge. You will not get the strength from looking outward. According to African wisdom, if a child's gift is not brought forth it becomes a poison. This poison prevents the development of full social potential in the community. So stay strong and true to your gift and as a community member, encourage others' gifts!
MARK

Imagine if we all saw ourselves and others from the perspective of this African wisdom.

Finding My Gift

- It's when you feel the "FLOW" (a.k.a in the zone, in the groove, on the ball).
- It makes you feel totally ALIVE!
- It is so natural and easy for you—just can't explain it.
- Time flies when you're doing it (8 hours feels like 15 minutes).
- You're not doing it for rewards. You do it because it makes you happy.
- Opportunities come out of nowhere for you when you're doing this.
- You help others when you do this.
- You're the only one who "hears the song" that fills you with ideas that can make a difference. No one hears it like you do. It's your special gift & true nature!

NINA'S GIFT:
COMPASSION

PRABHA'S GIFT:
SELF-AWARENESS & AWARENESS
OF OTHERS

Ideas About My Gift

Use this space to freely express yourself, through words or art, to remember when you have felt totally alive or in the "flow". What did it feel like for you? What was it about these experiences that made you feel so good? Have you seen any of these qualities pop up in other situations too?

Go to www.authentichappiness.com and try the "Signature Strengths Questionnaire" to get some ideas about your gift.

Checking back in:

→ When we take the time to know ourselves, we can make better choices that lead to happiness.

→ How we THINK, FEEL, and ACT (or REACT) work like gears—each influences the other.

→ Our thoughts can be intentional (we consciously choose them) or they can run on autopilot (we unknowingly repeat the same ones over & over).

→ Sometimes we resort to Monkey Mind, when our distorted thoughts hijack our common sense.

→ Emotions are our Inner Guidance System; like a compass, they tell us which direction to head.

→ Our emotions are like icebergs, if we don't address the deeper feelings concealed below the surface, we become frozen and rigid, in constant fear of cracking to pieces.

→ Emotions are physical: They are bio-chemicals running through our bodies.

→ When we get to know our feelings and welcome each of them as guests in our home, we can befriend them rather than live in fear of them.

→ The best part of getting to know ourselves is figuring out the unique gift(s) we were born with to share with our community & the world!

IV

SELF-MASTERY

"We must be the change we wish to see in the world."

-Mahatma Gandhi

Aikido 合気道

Aikido is a Japanese martial art that helps practitioners master their mind, body, and ki (life energy). By not flaring up into anger and reaction, the Aikido Master is able to master of all the energies at play, starting with his/her own. Rather than matching force with force, he/she blends with the motions of the attacker in order to redirect their momentum. This requires less energy and also helps to protect the attacker from injury. For this reason, Aikido is a about mastering oneself, not harming others.

We may not be an Aikido Master, but we are all on the journey to personal mastery. Where are you? Do you feel in control of or at peace with your thoughts, feelings and actions? What techniques do you use to handle people, things, or events that challenge your well-being??

On the Path to Self-Mastery

Here, There, or Somewhere In Between

CHOICE

Flying by the seat of your pants.

VS.

Choosing to be in the driver's seat.

AWARENESS

Denying & suppressing your negative thoughts & emotions.

VS.

Accepting & not judging your negative thoughts & emotions.

MENTAL & EMOTIONAL DISCIPLINE

Unconsciously REACTING to what life throws your way.

VS.

Understanding when and why you feel bad & using tools to learn how to ACT instead of REACT.

INTERDEPENDENCE

Only considering your own happiness.

Considering other's happiness too by taking responsibility for the impact of your actions on others.

Where are you on the journey?

OR ARE YOU SOMEWHERE IN BETWEEN?

The Development of "Self"
Checking the Ingredients

We've actually been on this path of Self-Mastery all along, so it should be no surprise to you! Since the day we were born, we've all been trying to figure out who we are, why we're here, and what we stand for. We've been given constant feedback from everyone and everything around us, every day of our lives: family, friends, teachers, coache, and even the media. These experiences have not only shaped our lives, but they've influenced our view of ourselves and what we think we believe in. Some people in our lives have fed and nourished us with positive messages, cultural values, and traditions, that have helped guide our actions. We can compare this to the comfort we feel with a hot bowl of healthy soup; there is a sense of security and identity every time you eat this soup. But what about the toxic messages that we've ingested that don't reflect who we really are or who we want to be? You know the ones from the media or friends who aren't really looking out for us. Or maybe they are simply the messages that once served us, but we've now outgrown. It's time to start making our own soup!

What's in your soup?

You can never be too rich or too thin.

You need to make sacrifices to get ahead.

No act of kindness is ever wasted.

Treat others the way you want to be treated.

Don't dream too big.

Where are your loyalties?

Love.

So you think you're college material?

Suck it up!

Date and marry within your culture.

Creating My Own Recipe

How would you change your soup recipe to include the ingredients for a happy and meaningful life? Throw into the pot the values, rituals, and beliefs that you cherish from your family, culture, friends and...

ADD the ingredients of your dreams! What do you need to live your happiest life? What would this soup look like, taste like, feel like, and smell like if there were no limits and if the only chef you had to answer to was yourself? This could be the best meal of your life.

Sous-Chef? Who would you hire to help you in the kitchen? Who will support you in this new recipe for happiness.

Love

Kindness

Follow your heart

Honesty

Where There's a Will There's a Way

It takes **courage** to look at your life, how you've become who you are, and who and what has contributed to your identity. Although this might seem daunting and scary to start blazing your own trail or playing around with new recipes for happiness, consider yourself **lucky** in that you are **beginning this quest now**, at this turning point in your life. Many people either never have the opportunity or **the will** to take on this life challenge or if they do, it's often not until their life is turned upside down. You can **start empowering your life** now with the **intention** to figure out who you are, make the **choice** to go for it, and then put it into **action**. If you have the will, anything is possible!

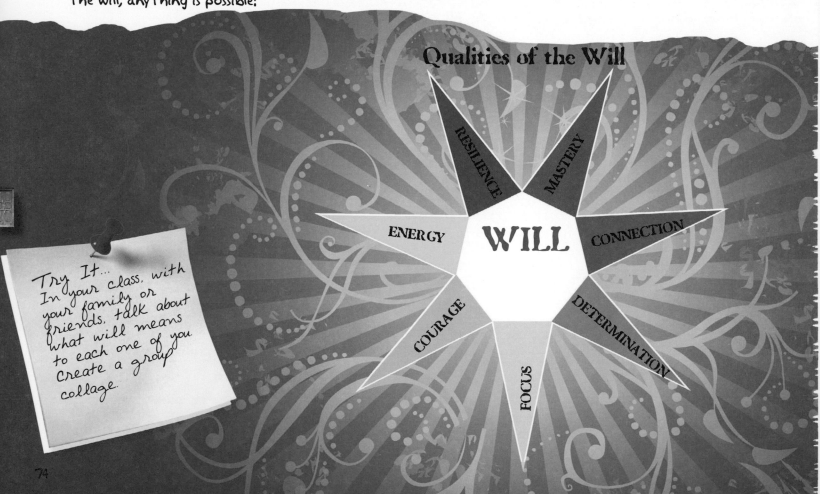

Qualities of the Will

WILL

RESILIENCE
MASTERY
ENERGY
CONNECTION
COURAGE
DETERMINATION
FOCUS

Try It...
In your class, with your family or friends, talk about what will means to each one of you. Create a group collage.

74

Finding My Will

Where do you look for your will? Some people feel like their will is found somewhere in their "gut". You know the place where you feel like you can find the power to do anything you believe in? The place where the good Samaritan goes to lift a car up with his bare hands to save a child. Or the place where Victor Frankl went to survive Nazi death camps or Thomas Edison went to create electricity even after failing with 9,000 experiments.

These types of examples can inspire us to overcome our self-pity, complaining, and desire to quit when faced with hardships along our journey. **We ALL have the will within us-we just need to figure out how to tap into it!** Perhaps these qualities might remind you of what your will feels like.

RESILIENCE	Athletes, you know the type of **intensity** that is required during the championship game versus a regular season game?
MASTERY	Musicians, you know the amount of **practice and skill** it takes to master your instrument or the **knowledge** needed to understand the theory behind your skill?
CONNECTION	Any student can appreciate the amount of **focus and concentration** that we need when we're trying to grasp a totally new and challenging subject...or a boring one!
DETERMINATION	You know when you're in the middle of a seemingly huge problem and there are many options to consider and you don't have a clue what to do? It takes **decisiveness** to be open to all of the alternatives, stick to a decision, and then not doubt yourself.
FOCUS	Anyone who has been bullied or tormented by others knows the amount of **tenacity** it takes to show up at school again. Or anyone who has failed or suffered serious challenges over and over and over again knows the type of **endurance** they need to keep on going.
COURAGE	When you're feeling the lowest of your lows and you have to "show up" somewhere–like give a speech, start a new school, apologize; it takes **guts!** Sometimes you need to be **bold**.
ENERGY	We all want to be part of a group, but deep down we also don't want to lose ourselves. It takes will to remain **connected with our true selves** first and then appreciate and connect with others.

We all have these qualities within us ready to draw upon. In one situation we might need to be courageous, while in another focus, is what will help get us through the day. As we tap into our will more often, we learn how to apply each of these qualities at the right time, in the right amounts, for the right reasons. It simply takes practice!

Finding My Will

Think back to a time when you remember using your will when you were faced with a situation that required something deep within you. It might have been a struggle, a big decision, a crossroad, helping someone, or even the risk of losing everything.

What do you remember about the situation? What did your will feel like? How would you describe the quality in you that helped you make it through? What did you learn about yourself? Write, rap, write a song. If you're an artist, draw your will.

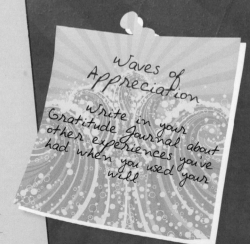

Waves of Appreciation

Write in your Gratitude Journal about other experiences you've had when you used your will.

TOOLS FOR SELF-MASTERY

As you continue on your path to **Self-Mastery & Happiness**, here are some tools that can support your journey.

1. Right on Target (p. 78-85)

- Reflecting on My World
- The Positive Power of Words
- Pushing My Buttons!!
- My Buttons
- Everything We Need Is Within Us
- Training Sessions
- Thoeun's Story

2. Nourish Yourself (p. 86-94)

- The Paralyzing Emotion
- Reflecting on Guilt
- Self-compassion
- Tree of Nourishment
- My Nourishment Plan
- Zone of Peace
- My Zone of Peace

3. Take the Armor Off (p. 95-99)

- Reflecting on My Armor
- We All Have Needs
- What We ALL Need
- An Open Mind & Heart

4. The Will to Understand (p. 100-104)

- The Will to Listen
- Active Listening–How To Do It!
- When We Both Have a Problem
- Try It…

"People who do not see their choices do not believe they have choices. They tend to respond automatically, blindly influenced by their circumstances and conditioning. Mindfulness, by helping us notice our impulses before we act, gives us the opportunity to decide whether to act and how to act."
Gil Fronsdal

Right on Target

Once we've committed to reflecting on our thoughts and feelings, we can then begin to look at our actions–what we say and do. Have you ever stopped to notice what words come out of your mouth? If your goal is to connect with others, support their happiness and your own, how often do you hit your target? Or do you sometimes miss altogether? Ask yourself...

Do my words hurt or harm?
Am I making things better or worse when I open my mouth every day?
Am I connecting people or am I alienating them from me and each other in what I say?
How good is my word? What energy do I give off in what I say and how I say it?
What kind of energy exchanges do I have with friends and family?
Am I exhausted or energized by those around me? What does that mean?

Words create worlds. They hold more power than we can ever imagine. We should all be VERY familiar with this power. Remember our Monkey Minds? What words still play out in your mind from your childhood? Are they hurtful or harmful? For example, as a child when you did something wrong were you told "How could you be so stupid?" or "It's okay, it's just a mistake. We all make them"? Do these words still hold power over you? What do you tell yourself today when you make a mistake? Using this as an example, we can compare our use of words to an archer lining up her arrow (words). A skilled archer takes her time to focus on the target (personal goals), taps into her will to choose the right technique (wise speech), and then takes action.

What's your goal? Happiness, achievement? Where are you aiming your words? Are they helpful or harmful in achieving your goal?

HELPFUL WORDS:
Aim for your mark (your goals).
It's okay if you miss, it takes practice!

HARMFUL WORDS:
Missing your mark is okay, but hitting someone in the back is not cool.

Reflecting on My World

What kinds of verbal exchanges are going on in your world (home, school, clubs, teams, friends)? What kinds of worlds are being created by these exchanges (welcoming, safe, friendly, exclusive, competitive, divisive)? At school, are you surrounded by: cliques, gossiping, bullying, isolation, stereotyping, lying, or humiliation? Track your conversations and even those around you for a day. Are they helpful or harmful?

How do these choices impact my happiness and others too?

Do you or the people you surround yourself with:

Exaggerate the truth to impress others?
Lie to avoid conflict or responsibility?
Constantly debate with others to win the battle?
Talk non-stop to avoid silence or facing feelings?
Thrive on creating drama?
Manipulate or avenge others with words?
How often do you wish you could take back what you said?

Our Journey

In Buddhism, we have to debate on the different topics of scripture. If you've ever seen one of these debating sessions you might really feel like that the monks were fighting with each other. There are often many different opinions so each opponent has to give many reasons to prove his argument.   Whoever is not able to prove his point is considered the loser. These debates are not the silly conflicts that we usually find in regular conversation. Here, they are not avoiding conflict they are just giving each other new ideas.
NGAWANG

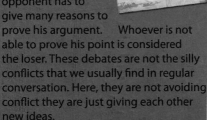

In search of true happiness we should be ethical and teach others ethical values so that one can have positive thoughts and live a happier life.
LHAMO

I think that the reason ethics is a necessity for promoting happiness because our actions shape the way we feel, and the way that people around us feel. If we cannot make ethical actions that lead to a positive outcome, then we are not promoting happiness for ourselves or the people around us who are being affected by our actions.
JOHN-NURI

The Positive Power of Words

What do you think of the power of speech? What difference does it make? Think of a time when someone spoke to you with respect, compassion, and genuine interest? What did it feel like? How did it impact your experience of happiness.

Waves of Appreciation

Write in your Gratitude Journal about a time someone inspired you with their speech

Pushing My Buttons!!!
What does this REALLY mean?

Boomerang Effect

Lose control

Lose friends

Lose inner peace

ANGER!

Lose yourself

Lose happiness

Feel regretful & embarrassed

Separate from others

REACT instead of ACT

Boomerang Effect

Let's all agree on one thing–**anger is NOT a bad thing!!** In small doses, it informs us that something's not right. Sometimes it can inspire us to stand up for ourselves, someone else, or just take the right action. The hot button we're talking about is the **anger that is more intense** and doesn't serve anyone. You know–**THAT button:** the one that someone or something pushes and it sends us **over the edge...it triggers us!** You know when you blast someone in a rage and then feel a huge sense of pride for defending your territory (a.k.a. caveman syndrome)? Then that relief of releasing your anger on someone else is soon replaced by a sense of **discomfort in your own skin.** You wish you could just rewind time, but you can't. Instead you're left with regret, embarrassment, and likely a broken relationship. This is because our level of happiness is closely connected to our relationships with others.

This is the destructive nature of **anger** 98 and there's **more than just one button involved!**

The biggest obstacle that prevents me from achieving happiness are anger and hatred. I am a person who easily gets angry, therefore this anger prevents me from making certain types of friends. When I feel hatred, it gives me a lot of stress in my mind and destroys my peace of mind.

DORJI

For me happiness is inner peace. If you have inner peace then there will definitely be happiness within you. So the root of happiness lies on being peaceful. We can prove this from the fact that His Holiness is a happy man because he is a peaceful man.

NGAWANG

Many people think that to be patient is a sign of weakness. I think that is a mistake. It is anger that is a sign of weakness.

THE DALAI LAMA

Our Journey

Happiness fully depends on one's way of handling the situation around him/her. One should control his/her inborn ability of anger, hatred, and envy. One needs to learn to tolerate the grief.
TSERING

I believe that it is our mental well-being that leads to strong positive actions. For example, in my life when I feel angry, my actions reflect this emotion. Therefore when I feel these feelings of anger, in my mind I make an ethical decision to deal with my anger and not suppress that feeling.
JOHN-NURI

It is said that when our minds master our actions and ethical thinking, this is the sole weapon to direct our action in promoting happiness and bliss. It's natural that we feel happy when we have done something good. Unethical actions trigger disasters that get you in trouble. So, yes, I agree that ethics govern our happiness.
DORGI

My Buttons...

ANGER = INNER PEACE

What pushes your buttons? Why? What happens when your buttons are pushed? Do you try to settle the score or think "pay back"? Anger cannot coexist with inner peace, they are opposing forces. What do you think? What else have you lost as a result of your anger?

Try It...

Watch how others around you handle their anger. Now that you know how much there is to lose, how do you view their choices?

Boomerang Effect

What goes around comes around. What you cause someone else to feel, will come back to you at some point in your life. What might that be?

Everything We Need Is Within Us!

Whether we believe it or not (our Tibetan friends do!), we have everything we need within us to not only with-stand pain and suffering, but to not lose compassion even for those who harm us. We might not be able to stop our buttons from being pushed, but we do have a choice about how we view our anger and how we deal with it. We can see anger as a tool to make a better decision and then take steps to work through it. Or we might see our anger as a threat to our happiness and let it take a hold of us, leading to choices that are poten-tially harmful to ourselves and others. What perspective do you take? Perhaps if we look back at some of these tools, we can tap into the wisdom and resilience that is within all of us…

Here are a series of archery tips to help you hit your target (happiness):

→ Remember the Guest House: notice when your negative thoughts and emotions are knocking at your door.

→ Whatever you do, don't ignore your emotion; don't deny or suppress them because they'll be starving later and might just pound your door down!

→ Check in with what each of these distressing emotions is trying to tell you (e.g. I feel threatened by this person, I'm afraid of failing, this exam is not fair).

→ Make a Choice: I'm going to be aware of these feelings and I'm going to choose a response that brings me happiness, not grief.

→ Find your Calm Center (don't get sucked into the twister): Hit the Pause Button, Walk Away, Breathe, Ground Your-self, etc.

→ Tap into your WILL, the place in your gut that gives you patience, determination, focus, energy, mastery, connection, and courage.

→ Think of the benefits of restraining your emotions–inner peace, compassion, friendship, happiness.

→ If needed, apply the Aikido philosophy and redirect your attacker's energy and save your own.

→ Adversity and those who harm us give us a chance to practice patience, self-discipline, and to define ourselves in relation to struggle.

→ Remember that those who act in anger towards us are also losing their inner peace, so have compassion for them.

→ Step outside yourself and think of the ripple effect your response will have on your own and others' happiness.

→ Choose a response that you can live with and not regret for years to come!

Practice, practice, practice so when REALLY difficult situation presents itself, you'll know what to do.

Training Sessions

1. Get a partner, a timer, a towel, and an ice cube. Hold the ice cube in the palm of your hand for as long as it's bearable (time it). Switch hands, then do it again, this time using a tip from above to deal with your "pain" (count breaths, tap into your will, think of the calm center of the twister, etc.). Switch partners.

Were your own times different? Why? What other observations did you make?

2. Apply the same tip and any others to the struggles you face over the next few days. Record the situations you were faced with, including the emotion and degree of the emotion (green, yellow, red), the tip you used, and what observations you made.

Situation/Emotion	Tip Used	Observations

BUNThoeun's Story
Gang Member to Peace Maker: You CAN Change

I worked for the remaining of my high school years at a copies and design shop. No girlfriends or hanging out. I had to help the family with my income. Plus, I was a shy guy. I didn't date until I was out of high school. That was when I had a girlfriend for about a year. Love was new and fresh to me.

One day, I lost patience because my girlfriend was taking a long time to put on her makeup. I nagged, but thought I was doing it out of love. When I got angry I yelled or threw tantrums. I reacted without thinking about the consequences. Eventually she couldn't stand my attitude and the way I expressed my anger and frustrations, so she cheated on me. I felt betrayed, so I did the only thing I knew, I blamed all my feelings on her. I woke up each morning, filled with anger and hatred. I found some comfort blaming everything on her, but I could not find inner peace within myself. Again, I dealt with my anger through drawing and video games, because nothing else seemed to relieve me of the pain. Then I realized that my pain was my own creation. I had to prove to myself that I could love again.

Over the years I met a few people who taught me. I met Randy Taran who introduced me to Dalai Lamas teachings on compassion, love, kindness, and patience. The idea of compassion was a wake-up call for me. I read his books and found ideas that would help me define my emotions. As soon as I learned not to blame others for my own actions and make myself accountable, I felt free. I was able to live with myself again.

2. Nourish Yourself

If we don't feel good on the inside, how can we respond in positive ways to changing circumstances on the outside? Life is unpredictable and constantly changing. The one guarantee is that we will all face struggle in our lives. When faced with these challenges we easily resort to old patterns.

I am BAD!

I'll NEVER get it right.

Stupid, stupid, stupid!!

I'm so SELFISH!!

I don't deserve ANYTHING good.

I am NOT WORTHY!

All we want though is to be happy, possibly figure out who we are, and maybe even gain some control over our lives. Not too much to ask!! If we look around at those people who do seem calm and centered, they have one thing in common–they take care of themselves. They nourish themselves from the inside out.

It is not selfish to take care of yourself! There is a big difference between constantly focusing on yourself and only your own needs at the expense of others versus doing things for yourself so you're happy. The first might be considered "Selfish," while the other is called "Taking Care of Yourself". Too many of us think the two interpretations are synonymous (Doing things for yourself = Selfishness). If you're not hurting anyone or causing them to "lose out" in the process, then do what you need to do to feel good. It's a gift for yourself and others. Everyone wins!!

Have you ever noticed how you interact with other people when you are happier?

Did you know? The heart pumps blood to itself first before it provides essential nutrients to the rest of the body. Be happy with yourself first! then you can make others happy.

The Paralyzing Emotion

When some of us try to take care of ourselves we are consumed with thoughts of unworthiness and even guilt. We don't think we deserve to take time to nourish ourselves or possibly even be happy. This feeling of guilt is even more intense when we make a mistake. Just like intense anger can chip away at our happiness, guilt is the most paralyzing emotion on our journey to happiness. It causes us to get stuck in not knowing what to do with our mistake and leaves us with a sense of despair rather than a desire for change or improvement. Instead of judging the act, we end up judging ourselves. This is self-defeating, disempowering, and doesn't help anyone. It's like turning anger back on ourselves, so now we're paralyzed and we've undermined any chance for inner peace.

Cultural Fact

• Your culture may or may not even have a name for guilt (Tibetans don't).
• They believe a person should acknowledge their mistake, deal with their own pain, confess to the right person, and then move on!
• Don't dwell on the mistake…doing nothing but dwelling helps no one.
• Instead, use your regret as basis for positive change.
• Commit to helping others, not harming them.

Remember the African wisdom about the gift? We are born with natural goodness. We are not inherently bad, we are inherently good. Plus, we ALL deserve happiness. Let's not forget it!

Our Journey

My definition of happiness is the "need to develop yourself". I am happy when I've done something that has changed myself for the better, something that will ultimately make others happier. I figure that the kinder person I am, the more I can contribute to others' happiness. For some reason, this seems really arrogant to me. Please let me know what you think.
JONJI

According to your question about your own happiness, you don't have to feel arrogant by feeling this way. Self-improvement is another way which we can find true happiness and bring happiness to others. Happiness does not just inherently happen. It develops within our hearts with respect to the environment we grow up in.
YANGCHEN

I believe that one's happiness is rooted in their inner peace. I feel at peace when I'm confident that my actions are making a positive impact within the global community, or just within my local community.
DANIEL

Reflecting on Guilt

Do you ever experience guilt? What does it feel like for you? Think of a past situation that involved a guilty feeling. Did it serve you well? If not, what would you have done differently, now knowing what you know?

So, we can learn from this Eastern perspective...

Don't beat yourself up!! It happened. It's done. It's OVER.

Acknowledge your mistake.

Accept your regret and inner grief. You're human!

Use your regret to motivate you to change next time.

Ask yourself, "What can I learn from this?"

Defining Moment: How will you define yourself as a result of this challenge?

Remember: You are pure goodness at the core. There is nothing wrong with you.

Nourish yourself – you deserve it!

Self-Compassion

Even when we feel angry, stuck, or guilty, there is always a way out. If a Lotus flower can grow in the mud, so can we! Our blossom can be found in our human capacity for compassion, starting with compassion for ourselves.

What Is Self-Compassion?

→ I notice when I'm hurting.
→ I feel empathy for myself when I recognize I'm struggling.
→ I'm understanding and kind to myself when I fail or make mistakes, rather than judgmental.
→ Rather than pitying myself when I'm having a hard time, I recognize that imperfection and failure are just a part of our human experience.
→ I'm motivated to help myself find a way out of struggle.

When we are able to find compassion for ourselves, we are then able to extend it to others. We all desire and deserve happiness so let's start by having compassion for ourselves along our journey!

Our Journey

How much energy are you willing to give others without expecting it back? There is a story that I was told in a church lesson. I don't have the exact story but it told about how everyone has a bucket with some water in it. Any time you are kind to someone you are adding water to their bucket from yours. Every time you are mean you are taking water from theirs to add to your bucket. The story talked about how some people protect their bucket from everyone, not willing to risk giving any to others because they cannot spare any, or people share too much of their water and have none for themselves, or people who take water from others to make their own bucket full. I liked that the story not only taught about the importance of giving but also taking care of yourself.

-KRISTEN

How would you describe your experiences with compassion, either when you shared it with someone else or someone shared some compassion with you? What did it look and feel like? What steps can you take to start being more compassionate with yourself?

Waves of Appreciation

Continue to write in your Gratitude Journal the times you were able to find compassion for yourself. What did you say or do? What impact did it have?

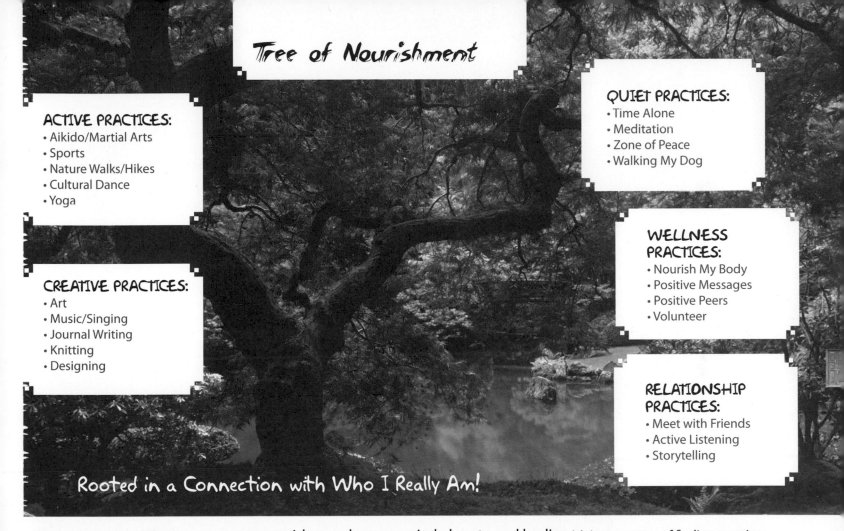

Tree of Nourishment

ACTIVE PRACTICES:
- Aikido/Martial Arts
- Sports
- Nature Walks/Hikes
- Cultural Dance
- Yoga

CREATIVE PRACTICES:
- Art
- Music/Singing
- Journal Writing
- Knitting
- Designing

QUIET PRACTICES:
- Time Alone
- Meditation
- Zone of Peace
- Walking My Dog

WELLNESS PRACTICES:
- Nourish My Body
- Positive Messages
- Positive Peers
- Volunteer

RELATIONSHIP PRACTICES:
- Meet with Friends
- Active Listening
- Storytelling

Rooted in a Connection with Who I Really Am!

There are so many different ways we **can nourish ourselves: our minds, hearts, and bodies.** It's just a matter of finding practices that bring us back to life and then making a plan to commit to them in our day-to-day life. To find practices that "fill you up," you might start by asking yourself: Do I re-energize by being alone or connecting with others? Am I in the "flow" when I create or when I compete? Do I take time each day to be "quiet"? What am I putting into my body? How do these items make me feel? Who am I choosing to hang out with? Do they fully support me? What do I want to do on a regular basis to reconnect with who I really am? What practices will support my journey to happiness?

MY Nourishment Plan

What practices fill you up and nourish you from the inside out? What feeds you and energizes you? What practices can you put into your daily or weekly life so you feel more peaceful on the inside?

Make a plan for yourself: try it and see what you notice (how do you feel?).

Practice	Plan (Frequency, Location, Time)	Observations

ZONE OF PEACE

Where do you go to find peace.

My Zone of Peace

Do you have a place or space where you can go to de-compress, chill out, re-energize, find yourself again, figure things out, regain perspective, or just find peace and quiet? It might be your room, a quiet and cozy nook in the attic, your favorite tree, or a secret spot by the ocean. It might even be a place in your mind that you visit when you close your eyes and just imagine. We call this a Zone of Peace – you might choose to call it something else. Regardless of what we call it, we just need to find one. We all need a place we can rely on, that is free from struggle, conflict and noise – to regroup and reconnect with ourselves on a regular basis. This is a big piece of nourishing ourselves.

Zones of Peace

At Home: Create a quiet space at home for everyone in your family to go and find peace.

At School: With your classmates and teacher, create a space in your classroom that is free from conflict. Come up with some "guidelines" about how to keep it a peaceful place or how you'll use it.

Draw, write, or imagine what does your Zone of Peace looks and feels like? What qualities does it have that help support you? If you don't have one, find one or create one!

Take the Armor off

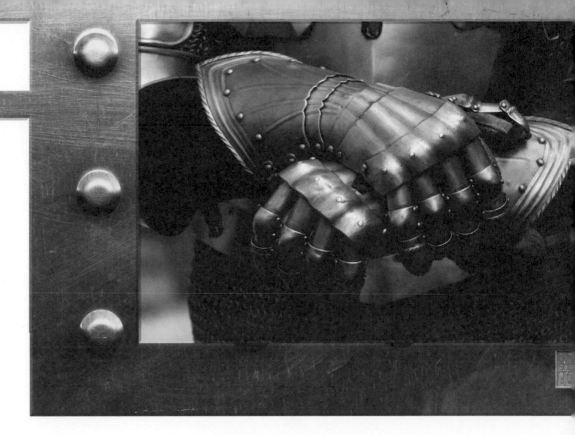

As we continue on our journey to find happiness, we are not alone. **Each and every one of us is on the same quest.** So why is it that we sometimes don't recognize that other people are also on their own journey? Rather than empathizing with others and our mutual journey, we sometimes distance ourselves from others, avoid them altogether, or sometimes even attack them.

It's like we're medieval knights when we:

1. Shield ourselves from others and any threat they pose to who we are or our happiness.
2. Hop on our high horse.
3. Armor up to defend ourselves at all costs.
4. Hastily strive to joust our attacker from their horse (and their quest for happiness).

This doesn't mean we need to expose ourselves to anything and anyone who threatens or challenges us. It's always healthy to have clear boundaries and expectations for how others treat us. We can make choices that respect our quest for happiness and that of others at the same time. This happens when we're less defensive and more open to engaging with others.

Take off the mask and your armor

• You might see that the person you're attacking has a **story too,** just like you do.

• His/her story, like the **links in the chain,** is made up of life experiences and conditioning that are connected to something that happened before (and some of it is painful).

• His/her actions are a projection of his/her story, not yours.

• It's not personal.

• You might realize that you're actually both fighting for the same thing—happiness.

Our Journey

When we begin to see ourselves as equals, all desires and struggles to conquer and dominate others will naturally disappear, leading to a peaceful world. I also want to add that we all have power to change things and situations around us. The problem is that many of us do not realize this. Because of this failure, we begin to struggle to be like others, and this is also the source of our unhappiness.
MERCY

What a wonderful thought: you think we all deserve happiness. You are right in saying this. Sometimes I feel very strange that we all deserve happiness because in real life we are doing more things which cause unhappiness than wonderful things which can create happiness. Why is our human heart more interested in learning bad things than good things? Why is it easier to make mistakes rather than to make a good contribution to society?
DONGBU

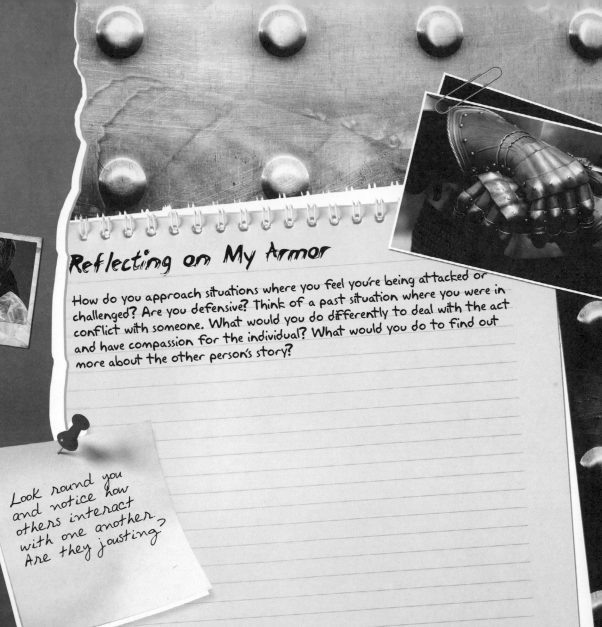

Reflecting on My Armor

How do you approach situations where you feel you're being attacked or challenged? Are you defensive? Think of a past situation where you were in conflict with someone. What would you do differently to deal with the act and have compassion for the individual? What would you do to find out more about the other person's story?

Look round you and notice how others interact with one another. Are they jousting?

We All Have Needs

We know that we are all united in our desire for happiness and wish to diminish suffering in our lives. We are also connected in our innate ability to feel compassion for one another. Our common humanity does not end there. In our human experience we all have needs, whether they are physiological or psychological they drive our motivations and our choices.

As we satisfy these needs in our life, we look to satisfy the next need up the pyramid. It all begins with survival; Do we have enough food and water? While some of us are worried about a conflict with a friend, others are worried if they'll eat today.

Did you know...
→ Every day, 800 million people go to bed hungry.
→ 1.2 billion people lack access to safe drinking water and 2.4 billion people lack access to proper sanitation facilities.

And then there are other young people around the world who have enough to eat, but don't know if they are safe.
→ Women and children account for 80 percent of civilian casualties during armed conflict.
→ An estimated 300 million children worldwide are subjected to violence, exploitation, and abuse.
→ Pregnancy is the leading cause of death for girls ages 15-19 in developing countries.

Maslow's Hierarchy of Needs

- Self-Actualization (being the best that I can be)
- Self-Esteem
- Love & Belonging
- Safety
- Survival (Food, Clean Water, Shelter)

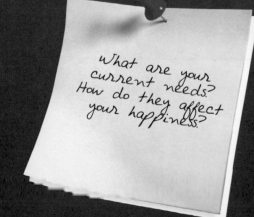

What are your current needs? How do they affect your happiness?

What We ALL Need

At the end of the day, we are all the same: We just want our needs met. By recognizing even this one similarity rather than our differences, we might view the circumstances and the people around us from a more compassionate angle. Rather than armoring up to defend ourselves in the you versus me battle, we might ask ourselves:

"I wonder what he/she needs?"

It's like we're taking the time to consider what is under the surface of someone's "iceberg". Everyone has their story and most of it is not visible to the eye. Whatever need is not being met in someone's story is motivating their choices. So, their choices are not about you; they're about the other person and his/her needs. By responding to others with compassion, an open mind, and a little bit of love, we are very likely going to fulfill the very needs they are missing. And what do you think will happen then? When we get our needs met, we can all move onto bigger and better things…and be happier at the end of the day! !

What we ALL need: Check your story

To be loved

To be accepted

To feel included

To belong

To feel like I matter

An Open Mind and Heart

Take time to consider someone else's story this week when you're faced with a struggle with them. Ask yourself, "I wonder what he/she needs? What's his/her story?" Track your interactions below: What exchanges took place? What emotions did you feel? How did your own emotions or actions change when you took time to listen or consider the other peron's story?

Waves of Appreciation

Write in your Gratitude Journal about the people who have helped you meet your needs.

The Will to Understand

What happens when we don't have the full story? Well, we either misunderstand what's real and true for someone else or we mind read and make assumptions about their story. Either way, the story becomes our truth, not theirs. It's like running on autopilot, but this time you're writing someone else's script. Instead, we might try to be more intentional in our thoughts and choose to be open to the idea that others have a story and needs too. Like any other situation where we don't know the answers, we just need to ask questions. Then, we allow others to speak their truth. This is possible when we use our will to understand others rather than control them.

The Will to Control
Selfishness—when we want to possess & dominate
Self-Centeredness—when we are only willing to see things from our own angle and we only want to do things our "own way"
Lack of Understanding—when we don't appreciate other people's needs or differences (race, gender, social class, religion, etc.)

VS.

The Will to Understand
Appreciation—when we appreciate our sameness in our universal quest and our differences
Empathy —when we are able to put ourselves in someone else's shoes
Courage—when we are bold enough to ask questions about other people's needs

In which direction do you want to focus your will? We can use our energy and determination to control our relationships with others or we can use our courage and connections to build our relationships.

The Will to Understand =
the will to recognize each person "as he/she is" and that he/she has the "right to be who he/she is".

The Will to Listen

At the end of the day, we all want to be understood. We all want to be accepted for who we are, exactly as we are. Regardless of our outer world, our age, gender, race, religion, the clothes we wear or the music we listen to, we all just want to be accepted for our inner world. At the core of our inner world are our feelings. When we feel understood, that our feelings are legitimate just as they are rather than right or wrong, then we are on the path to happiness.

Are you willing to fully accept others and their feelings? Do you have the will to listen?

The next time someone shares a need or problem with you:

DO
This is Active Listening:
- Understand their feelings
- Accept that feelings are always legitimate, not right or wrong
- Notice the attitudes & feelings in the message given
- Tell the person as exactly as you can what you heard them say (attitudes and feelings)

DON'T
These are Roadblocks:
Advise
Lecture
Blame
Label
Analyze
Divert
Threaten

"Listening is such a simple act. It requires us to be present, and that takes practice, but we don't have to do anything else. We don't' have to advise, or coach, or sound wise. We just have to be willing to sit there and listen."
Margaret J. Wheatley

Active Listening-How To Do It!

We can all get our needs met if we start from a place of honoring each of our needs, expressing our needs, and listening to what the other person needs.
Try these tools. It takes practice, but it's SO worth it:

Active Listening-How To Do It!

When SOMEONE ELSE has a problem with me:
(Just accept their feelings!)

• Focus on the OTHER person and get yourself out of the way.
• Do not respond with your own ideas (your opinion, logic, evaluation, analyzing, etc.)
• Try to imagine what they're feeling.
• Try saying:

You feel _____ about _____
I guess you feel _____
It sounds like you feel _____
Let me see if I understand; you feel
_____
I'm not sure I'm with you, but
_____

Then just listen. You don't need to advise or measure or solve their problem!

How to give an I-Message

When I have a problem with someone else:
(Help them understand and accept your feelings.)

• Avoid "YOU" messages that blame and accuse the other person. This method fails to change the behavior you're not happy with, and it just makes the other person defensive (remember the armor?).
• Say "I" messages instead (let them know what you feel):

I feel _____ when you _____
because _____ (explain the effect their choices have on you–what you lose).

Perhaps you can help the other person actively listen to you by suggesting:

I just need you to listen right now. I don't need you to solve my problem or offer advice.

Then listen if they need to express their point of view too!

When WE BOTH have a problem:
(There's a conflict between us)

Define the Problem:
• Use "I" Messages to state your need.
• Active Listen to make sure you understand their need.

Brainstorm Solutions:
• Be open
• Don't judge
• Think win/win
• Active listen if feelings come up

Choose A Solution:
• Evaluate ideas (what will work vs. not work)
• Don't criticize ideas
• Choose one or more solutions that you can both "live with".

Try It:
• Who will do what by when?
• Make a commitment to try the solution(s).
• Check in with each other to see if you liked this process.
• Check in later to see if the solution(s) worked.

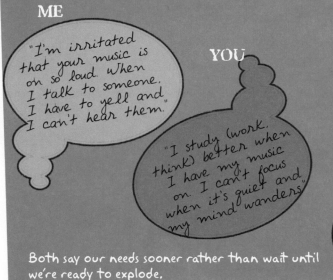

ME
"I'm irritated that your music is on so loud. When I talk to someone, I have to yell and I can't hear them."

YOU
"I study (work, think) better when I have my music on. I can't focus when it's quiet and my mind wanders."

MY NEED
To be able to have conversations so I can talk without yelling and can hear the other person

YOUR NEED
To be able to focus on what your doing

Both say our needs sooner rather than wait until we're ready to explode.

POSSIBLE SOLUTIONS:

• Turn the music down a litte
• Go somewhere else to have a conversation
• Wear headphones
• Agree on times when it's okay to have music loud
• Agree to turn it down when other person has someone over or is on the phone
• Go to separate rooms
• Get earplugs

CHOOSE SOLUTION (S) AND ASK: WILL THIS WORK FOR BOTH?

I can go downstairs to make a call sometimes.

I'll need some new headphones - I'll go get some tomorrow.

I could wear my headphones when I want it really loud.

When you're not here, I can turn it up as loud as I want.

Try it...

Rather than blaming or accusing someone when you have a problem with them, try letting them know what you need and help them undersand and meet your needs. Let them know....

1. What you're feeling (e.g., angry, ticked off, frustrated, disappointed, hurt, jealous...)
2. When you felt this way (let them know which specific actions/behaviors made you feel this way).
3. How their choices affected you in a negative way (explain to them how you're losing out.).

Then try **active listening** with this person or someone else who has a problem with you. No roadblocks, just an open ear. The only thing you need to do is sit back and acknowledge their feelings. It's not personal remember.

What did these experiences feel like for you? You can write or sketch.

Waves of Appreciation

Write in your Gratitude Journal about the times you chose to actively listen to someone. What did it feel like? How did the other person respond?

Just a Moment...

Throughout our journey to Self-Mastery and happiness we experience many different moments. Some push our buttons, some are inspiring, some are boring, some are wild, some are calm, some are just crummy. Each moment, good, bad, bright, or sad is filled with an opportunity to get a little bit closer to knowing who we are, closer to that place where we can feel calm in the center of any storm. Sometimes we take a couple steps up the up the staircase and the next moment we tumble back down to the bottom. This is the human experience!

One way to look at our lives, the good and the challenging stuff, is to think of life as bite-sized moments rather than a handful of significant events, either past or future, which decide who we are or who we will become. We have an opportunity to start fresh each new moment. Each moment is a new now and the good thing is that now repeats itself over and over again. Forget about past, present, and future, just think now. So we didn't make the best decision now then we'll try the next moment, the next now. We can pat ourselves on the back when we get a nice string of positive moments in a row! When we mess up on a few moments, don't fret simply start fresh the next moment. This is **DOABLE!!**

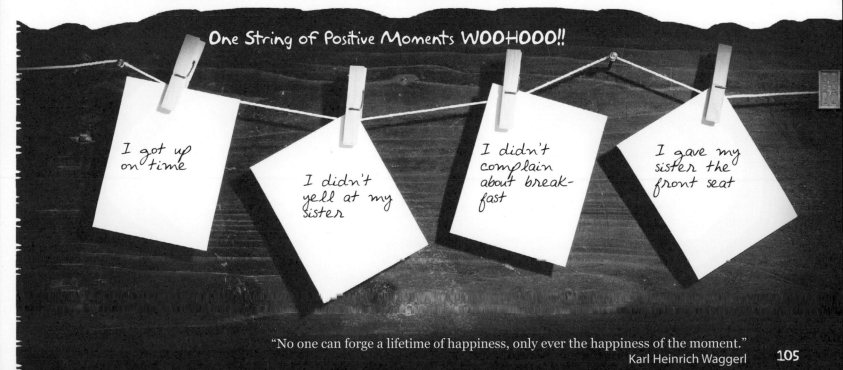

One String of Positive Moments WOOHOOO!!

I got up on time

I didn't yell at my sister

I didn't complain about break-fast

I gave my sister the front seat

"No one can forge a lifetime of happiness, only ever the happiness of the moment."
Karl Heinrich Waggerl

What Do I NOW Know about happiness?

How can I put this into action in my life?

"Until one is committed, there is hesitancy, the chance to draw back, always ineffective-ness. Concerning all acts of initiative and creation, there is one elementary truth, the ig-norance of which kills countless ideas and splendid plans: that the moment one definitely commits oneself, then providence moves too. All sorts of things occur to help one that would never otherwise have occurred. A whole stream of events issues from the decision, raising in one's favor all manner of unforeseen incidents, meetings, and material assistance which no man could have dreamed would have come his way."

W. H. Murray, of the Scottish Himalayan Expedition

Checking back in:

→ Self-Mastery is about becoming the person you really want to be.

→ We can use our WILL (mastery, connection, determination, focus, energy and resilience) to live our best life.

→ We need to look at our actions (what we say & do) so we can make choices that bring us happiness.

→ Words are powerful. They can help or harm.

→ We can handle adversity if we nourish ourselves.

→ Anger & guilt take us away from happiness.

→ Self-compassion can help resolve any struggle!

→ A Zone of Peace is a place where we can find peace and calm.

→ Instead of defending ourselves from others, we might take our armor off and see our mutual search for happiness.

→ We all have needs & just want them to be met.

→ We can control others or understand them.

→ We'd all be happier if we actively listened.

Choose supportive friends

Interview inspiring people

#

Let your frustration out in an email then DON'T send.

Visualize a great day   Make a "Dream Board" – a collage of how you WANT to live your life. Look at it every day.

V

COMPASSION IN ACTION

"It is not the *magnitude* of our actions but **the amount of love** that is put into them that matters"

—Mother Theresa

What Would You Do?

>You are having the **worst day** and then your best friend ignores you.

>You studied for hours and still **didn't get the grade** you had hoped for on your exam.

>Your bother is a basketball fnatic; he just find out he **didn't make the team.**

>**On** your way to lunch with your friends, the shy guy at school who never seems to fin in is knocked ot he ground by one of your friends.

>While waiting in the emergency room at the hospital you see a **young girl sobbing.**

>You are **already late for** your appointment and an elderly lady trips and falls on the sidewalk in front of you.

>**One** of your closest friends confides in you about a **se-rious problem** (eating disorder, thoughts of suicide) and asks you to keep it a secret.

Ways of Caring

DISCONNECTED — CONNECTED — OVER-CONNECTED

"I don't care, that's your problem."	"It sounds like you were really hurt by that."	"That's brutal! I feel so bad for you!"

→ "I don't see what you're feeling." → Don't get involved! → Lack of interest or concern.	→ "I see what you're feeling." → I am concerned; I can help you and maintain my own feelings.	→ Over involvement with emotions of the other person – "I feel what you feel." → I'm lost in your pain.
APATHY	**EMPATHY**	**SYMPATHY**

Many of us hang out at either ends of the caring spectrum...

DISCONNECTED (Apathy): When we just don't get involved (with others and even with ourselves). Sometimes it's easier that way   it's less risky and doesn't require an emotional commitment on our part. At the same time, it can also get quite lonely living from this perspective.

OVER-CONNECTED (Sympathy): When we get way too attached to other people's pain. It's as though we've morphed our body into the other person's and merged with their heart. Of course its kind to care, but it really doesn't help anyone when we're disabled by someone else's suffering.

The best place to hang out is somewhere in the middle...

CONNECTED (Empathy): When we can recognize someone else's pain, yet maintain our own separate feelings. We can put ourselves in someone else's shoes... but we bring our bodies with us. We learn to care and be strong.

Checking out Connections

Look around you and notice your family, your classes, your group of friends. How connected are the people in these groups? What do you notice about how they interact with one another? Are they connected, disconnected, or overconnected? What about you?

Apathy

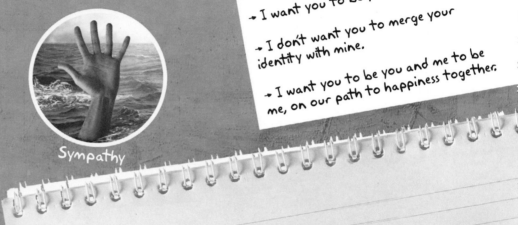
Sympathy

Thanks for your sympathy, but I need your empathy.

→ I want you to pay attention to me, know that I am sad, but I don't want you to sit and be immersed in sadness with me.

→ I want you to be you.

→ I don't want you to merge your identity with mine.

→ I want you to be you and me to be me, on our path to happiness together.

Empathy

The Road to Compassion

Before we can show compassion to someone in need,
we first need to recognize their pain (empathy).

EMPATHY - RECOGNIZE IT!

> We understand what it's like to walk in somone else's shoes: We recognize their pain.

> For example: We are easily able to recognize our friend's hurt in their eyes, body language, and tone of voice.

DO it

COMPASSION IN ACTION - DO IT!

> Once we recognize someone else's pain, we can choose to TAKE ACTION! We feel the desire to help the person in some way, to help relieve their pain.

> For example: We choose to sit and listen to their sadness, even when it's hard and we don't know what to say. We can be there for them.

RECOGNIZE it

What is Compassion (in Action)?

It's necessary for our survival. In the first 24 hours of life we depend on the physical care, love and affection of our caregivers.

It's a biological emotion that every human being has the ability to feel ... it's within ALL of us.

It comes from the heart, AND requires some thought: What's the best choice I can make to help and empower this person in need?

It involves no expectation of reward or praise.

It sometimes takes a lot of courage
(Letting someone know about a friend who's in danger).

It's sharing hope instead of pity, knowing that if circumstances were different it could have been you.

And if you can't show compassion (make things better) at the time, then at least don't make it worse. When someone trips and you don't have a band aid, then at least don't laugh.

Did you know?

The Hebrew term for compassion is rahum which comes from the word rehem meaning womb. Well, this is where we first experience compassion after all!

Reflecting on Compassion

What is your personal understanding of the term compassion? Some people think compassion is weakness, while others believe it is strength. What do you think? Why?

Can you think of a past situation where you chose to do something to help someone in need? What did you do and what did it feel like?

Simple Ways to Show Compassion:

* Actively listen
* Spend time together
* Cook a meal
* Pick up groceries
* Be present

waves of Appreciation

In your Gratitude Journal write about seeing an act of compassion

113

Bumthoeun's Story:

The Car Accident

I was in the middle of a meeting, when I heard loud noises. I sushed outside to see a man stomping the windshield of my car. Broken glass scattered everywhere. My hands began to tremble. My mouth dropped. In the midst of the chaos and confusion I recognized his face. I know him from high school. As he was walking away, I followed him, shouting, " What's wrong with you!?"

A Face from the Past

He stopped, tunred around. I could see the shock in his eyes. Marvin stared at me, and after a few seconds I could see some tears forming in his eyes. Standing on both sides of him were his older brother and his buddy. His buddy continued to poke Marving, telling him to "knock him out." I was stepping back to prepare for a punch but then my entire staff showed up behind me. He hesitated and walked away, while we called the police to arrest him.

Marvin's Story: The will to Understand

About 5 minutes later the police officer arrived, handcuffed him, and threw him into the backseat of the cruiser. Mean while, his brother was pleading and begging me not to press charges and offered to pay for the damages whtin a week. I was filled with anger and thoughts of revenge–not empathy. At that moment Marving told me why he was upset; his mother had died. Upset, Marvin decided to get drunk and hop onto a bus, not caring where it would lead him. As he stepped out of the bus, he tripped, falling on his face and chipping a tooth. In a rage, he immediately released his anger out on my car without thinking about the onsequences.

Finding Connection-Finding Empathy

After hearing his story, I tried to put myself in his situation. Yes, I was upset, angry, and shocked with disbelief that this could be happening to me. But I also had to decide whether I would throw this man in jail for getting a little worked up after his mother's death and a bunch of bad luck, or give him his freedom and help him learn a valuable lesson on how to control his anger in the future.

Compassion in Action

I asked the officer to release Marvin. I realized that no harm was done to me, only to my car. I could tell Marvin was grateful. I asked him to promise me to think before he lets his emotions control his actions. I felt sincerity in his trembling voice, when he uttered the word "Yes." He was also calm knowing he was a freed man. One week later, Marvin's brother came into my office and handed me a bundle of cash. He looked at me with a smile and said, "Thank you for waht you did. I hope that we didn't cause you too much trouble." I could tell that he was very sorry also.

Making a Choice

I chose to believe that even with or without money, forgiveness is the right thing to do. I did it to find peace within myself. Being reimbursed for the repair was good, inner peace is more valuable than a broken windshield and it was something that both Marvin and I had because I decided to chose empathy over revenge.

Bunthoeun Hack

Our Journey

Universal Responsibility is about all our actions being motivated purely out of deep concern for others. I agree with this, but I know also that this is very difficult. Please, can any of you share your experience with me on how my actions can be motivated by concern for others?
PATIENCE

When we are faced with inevitable choices and decisions, it is good to consider and act in a way which is less harmful and above all, more beneficial, not just to ourselves, but to others as well. Do not be in a hurry to decide or to act. Take it easy, think about the choices and options available, and then go for that which will promote goodness and benefit others.
EMMANUEL
Teacher - Nigeria

Reflecting on Genuine Compassion

Who are you compassionate towards? Are you excluding anyone? Why?
Like Theon, the challenge is showing compassion to people who've hurt us. Is this even possible? Why/Why not?

Discuss It
As a family, group, or class, identify people who you think have displayed compassion even for people who've harmed them. What have they taught us?

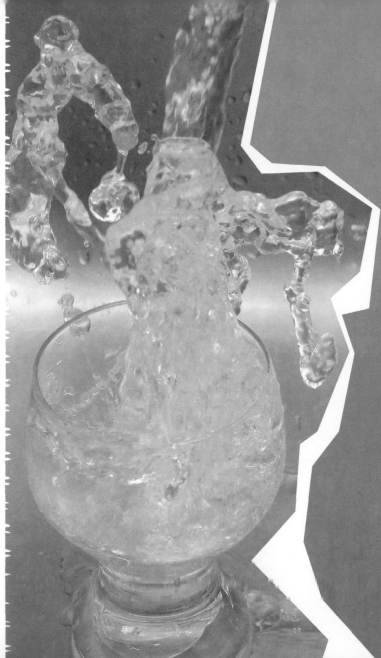

Where do We Start?

Compassion is like filling up cups!

We can start by filling up our own cup, first by recognizeing our own needs (empathy) and then showing ourselves kindness, understanding, acceptance, and forgiveness (compassion).

Once our own cup is full, it naturally overflows into other cups. It's not until our own cup is full, (when we accept ourselves just the way we are, with warmth and understanding), what we can extend some compassion to others.

As compassion fills and flows from one cup to another we realize that our cup never really empties when we experience the joy of taking care of ourselves and sharing compassion with others.

Fill your cup first! Practice self-compassion and it will extend to others!

How Full Is Your Cup?

How full is your cup?
How much understanding, kindness and acceptance do you have for yourself?

How often do you feel this way?

Almost Never				Almost Always
1	2	3	4	5

Complete each survey by rating each situation. Add up the score for each survey, separately, then look at the bottom for the value of your score.

Survey 1:

_____When something painful happens I tend to blow the situation out of proportion.

_____I'm critical about my own flaws and inadequacies.

_____When I'm feeling down I tend to focus on and obsess about everything that's wrong.

_____When I'm feeling down, I think that everyone else is happier than I am.

_____When I think about my flaws, it tends to make me feel more separate and cut off from the rest of the world.

_____When times are really difficult, I tend to be tough on myself.

0 - 10 = IMPRESSIVE
11 - 20 = ON THE RIGHT TRACK
21 - 30 = YOU DESERVE MORE

Survey 2:

_____When something painful happens I try to keep things in perspective.

_____I try to be understanding and patient towards those parts of my personality I don't like.

_____When something upsets me I try to keep my feelings in balance.

_____When I'm down and out, I remind myself that there are plenty of other people feeling like I am.

_____When I feel inadequate in some way, I try to remind myself that everyone feels this way at times.

_____When I'm going through a very hard time, I give myself the caring and understanding I need.

0 - 10 = YOU DESERVE MORE
11 - 20 = ON THE RIGHT TRACK
21 - 30 = IMPRESSIVE

119

* Based on self-evaluation (successes and failures).
* A comparison or competition - you don't have to feel better THAN others to feel good about yourself.
* Dependent on outside circumstances in your life.

Check the ones that sound familiar:

○ I am the **ONLY** one struggling here.
○ No one else is suffering like me.
○ My struggles are **HUGE!**
○ I don't have time to consider someone else's pain.

○ If I'm too nice to myself, I'll let myself get away with anything.
○ I'll just lounge on the couch today.
○ Bring on anything that makes the pain go away.

○ Yeah, I like myself.
○ I stand out from the crowd.
○ I'm prettier/smarter/better than him/her.
○ I rock! I just aced my exam.

Self-Pity

Am I lost in my own drama?

Although you might be considering your own pain, you get so wrapped up and blinded by it that you totally disconnect from others and their pain.

Self-Indulgence

Is this making me stronger?

Quick pleasure fixes might feel good at the time, but in the long run they often hurt your health. Besides, when you avoid facing what hurts, you're postponing taking charge of your life.

Self-Esteem

When am I happy with myself?

Although you think you care about yourself, you're always judging yourself based on the constantly changing circumstances around you. If you fail, you feel bad about yourself. If you succeed, you feel good. In reality, you're important no matter what your grades are or how great you look that day.

What Self-Compassion IS...

* A choice and within my control.
* How I choose to look at situations (In a way that makes me feel better, not worse).
* Being kind to myself, just because I'm on this planet, not because I did something perfectly.
* Accepting myself exactly as I am, with human imperfections and all.
* Being gentle on myself when I'm not proud of who I am.
* Forgiving myself when I've put myself in a situation where I need to learn from my mistakes.

What do you think Self-Compassion is? What does it look like and feel like to you?
If the benefits are so great, why is it so hard for us to be self-compassionate?

Waves of Appreciation

Each night this week, write one way you were self-compassionate during the day.

Judgment

Never good enough

Inadequacy

Failure

Loss

Not getting what I want

Comparison

Let's face it – the trip down the river of life is not always a smooth ride. It is packed with jagged and unforgiving rocks, both visible and below the surface. The sooner we come to this realization, rather than resist it, the calmer our ride will be, the more self-compassionate we'll be and the more we'll be able to go with the flow. Whether we like it or not, we're ALL headed down the river so we might as well pack the right supplies:

1. Self-kindness that might offer us some gentleness when we're heading straight for the next boulder.

2. Mindfulness about our emotions so we accept them, rather than deny or exaggerate them.

3. The acceptance of our **common humanity** - that we're ALL heading down stream. No one's ride is going to be perfect.

BE PREPARED!

Mindfulness

Self-kindness

Common Humanity

122

Packing for the Ride

What will you pack for your ride down the river so you may be more compassionate towards yourself as you head for the next boulder or are upside-down midstream?

Try It!

With your family, class or group, share stories of how you've been self-compassionate, either in thoughts or actions.

Compassionate Communication

Once we get a handle on being compassionate towards ourselves, we can begin to extend it to others. When we think of Compassion in Action, we often imagine physical acts of kindness or thoughtful gestures. Probably the most powerful way we show compassion, though is not so visible and something we engage in every day - conversations. Compassionate Communication is a way of speaking and listening that connects us with ourselves and with each other in a way that allows our natural compassion to flow. When we move away from old habits of judging, blaming and analyzing others to developing a deeper awareness of each of our needs (like survival, safety, love and belonging, self-esteem), life gets better.

Communication Style:
BLAME & JUDGMENT

* Tools: Blame, insult, compare, label, evaluate ourselves & others
* View: Good vs. bad, right vs. wrong, you vs. me
* Avoid: Responsibility for our thoughts, feelings & actions
* Look: Outside ourselves
* Excuse: I didn't have a choice
* What others hear: Criticism
* Response from others: Self-defense & counterattack

Communication Style:
COMPASSION & RESPONSIBILITY

* Tools: Respect, empathy, attention
* View: We all just want our needs met
* Avoid: Alienating each other
* Look: Inside ourselves for what we feel, need and expect
* No Excuses: The choice is mine
* What others hear: We all have needs
* Response from others: Compassion

"Out beyond ideas of wrong and right, there is a field. I'll meet you there."
RUMI

How to Communicate Compassionately

It all comes down to realizing that we all have stories… attitudes and armor that we use to protect ourselves from unmet needs. Compassionate communication is about putting aside the armor of self-defense and what we think someone might think about us, and instead, listening past the story someone is telling to the real stuff… to what that person actually needs. We don't have to give up our needs… compassionate communication is the best way to get what we all want and need. The problem is that most of us have never been taught to think about what we need. Instead, we're taught to think about what's wrong with the other person. The funny thing is that when we are able to express what we need, we have a better chance of getting our needs met. As we value and meet our needs, we can encourage and help others to do the same.

HONESTLY EXPRESSING..
who I AM without blaming or criticizing
(Just the FACTS & what YOU feel and need)

LISTENING DEEPLY…
to who YOU ARE without hearing blame or criticism
(Don't react… just try to understand the deeper story)

"When I hear/see you _____, I feel_____ because _____."

"My hope for myself is, and for you is ____. Do you think you could try ____?"

"Your hope is _____. Would you like me to _____?"

"When YOU hear/ see me _____, you feel_____ because _____."

125

Tracking My Conversations

Observe your conversations for one day this week. How are you responding to your friend's or family's needs? How are you expressing your own needs to your friends or family? What felt right? What didn't?

Person	Dialogue (words you exchanged)	How it Felt

Acceptance... for What's Below the Surface

When the power of love overcomes the love of power the world will know peace.
Jimi Hendrix

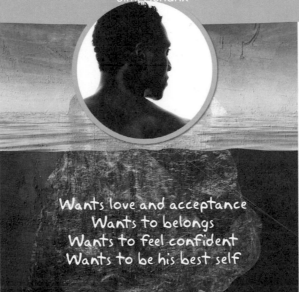

Wants love and acceptance
Wants to belongs
Wants to feel confident
Wants to be her best self

Wants love and acceptance
Wants to belongs
Wants to feel confident
Wants to be his best self

Wants love and acceptance
Wants to belongs
Wants to feel confident
Wants to be his best self

When we start recognizing the impact our choices have on others, we might start feeling a closer connection with the people we come in contact with… or at least take more responsibility for the choices we make. Making better choices begins with taking the time to look below the 10% we see on the surface of other people's lives. Rather than apathetically disconnecting from others based on our sweeping assumptions, judgments and intolerances of their hairstyle, clothing or skin color, or just thinking that we are so different, we might look deeper to who they really are as a fellow human being, by considering what we actually have in common.

Ultimately, we all have the same needs. When we care enough to ask questions, we recognize that although we are each diverse, we are united in our pursuit of happiness and need for acceptance and belonging. Through this compassionate lens, we can start accepting others exactly as they are. We can also take responsibility for the choices we make, especially in our interactions with them. We might actually engage with people we normally wouldn't. We might care more or argue less. We might let go of the power and need to control other people's lives, possibly confront our discomforts with unfamiliar cultures or groups, and release our expectations about how everyone needs to live in accordance with our own personal values. Our own happiness does not come from expecting others to change who they are to make us feel happy, but rather it's about feeling the joy of accepting everyone we encounter exactly as they are. This is genuine compassion… the choice that fills all of our cups and leads to genuine happiness.

Reflecting on My View of Others

We always have a choice in how we interact with people. We can choose power, apathy, empathy, acceptance, compassion. Do I choose to connect or accept this person as s/he is? Or am I choosing to disconnect or disregard him/her and his/her needs? Do I bring out the best in him/her or the worst? What choices have you made in your interactions with others... step back and observe yourself and the effects you create in other people's lives.

Try it...
Try to look below the surface of someone's life and find out more about who the really are (especially someone who you might have an assumption about). What do you find out?

Developing Diversity Consciousness

Being accepting and compassionate towards others, regardless of gender, race, religion or lifestyle, is no small feat. We all have the capacity to feel compassion, but extending it to the stranger on the street or the person on the bus who speaks an unfamiliar language, requires an open mind. Genuine compassion is a learned skill that grows when we develop a new understanding and awareness of diversity and how we interact with others who are different than ourselves. We call this diversity consciousness, which is a learning process...

6. Following Through:

Do I actively and compassionately listen to others? Do I reflect on my interactions with others?

1. Examining Myself & My World:

What do I hide below the surface? Who am I? What do I know about my culture? Can I be objective?

2. Expanding My Knowledge of Others & their Worlds:

Connect with someone from another culture: What do you have in common? What's different?

Diversity Consciousnes

5. Checking Up On Myself:

What assumptions and judgements do I make about others? Who am I comfortable with? Who am I not comfortable with? Do I question and evaluate these choices?

4. Uncovering How We Treat Each Other:

Do I see inequality in my own or other cultures (gender, race, class)? What privileges do I have? Did I earn them?

3. Stepping Outside Myself:

Try to put yourself in someone else's life (live their life for a day). Interview others or read personal stories.

129

What's Your Plan?

What stage are you at in your development of diversity consciousness (1, 2, 3, 4, 5 or 6)?
What steps can you (or your class/group) take this week (or this month) to expand your understanding of a culture (your own or another)?

Date	Plan	Observation

He prayed - it wasn't my religion.
He ate - it wasn't what I ate.
He spoke - it wasn't my language.
He dressed - it wasn't what I wore.

He took my hand - it wasn't the color of mine.
But when he laughed - it was how I laughed.
And when he cried - it was how I cried.

AMY MADDOX- as quoted in Teaching Tolerance Magazine

TOP 10 LIST

1. Address people the way they want to be addressed
(Many Native Americans identify with their tribe: Navaho, Sioux...)

2. Keep an open mind
(Be open to different views of a situation and question your assumptions)

3. Actively Listen and Communicate Compassionately

4. Check understanding
(Ask for clarification: "Do I need to explain further?" or "Does that make sense?" or for yourself "Is that idea like...?")

5. Do some research
(Before interacting with a new group, find out about them: library, internet, ask a friend, etc.)

6. Think through what you are going to say before you say it
(How are you going to address someone?)

7. Avoid slang or ethnic jokes
(Someone will feel excluded).

8. Use as many different styles of communication as possible
(Visual aids, sign language, draw a picture...)

9. Be conscious of how fast you are talking
(Repeat yourself if you need to)

10. Do not assume that you can or should ignore differences
(Let's celebrate our differences!)

The simplest step we can take is to communicate with others who are different than us in ways that are inclusive and compassionate.

Finding Forgiveness

Probably one of the most significant emotions connected with compassion is forgiveness. How do we show someone understanding and kindness when they've hurt us? How do we give love and acceptance when it feels like we're getting the opposite in return? Not easy. Instead, we often cling tightly to words or actions that have hurt us. We do this by blaming the person who hurt us and then creating a grievance story (you know, the one where you give the offender the power and you're the victim?).

When we take a closer look at what forgiveness really means, perhaps we can start to let go of our grievance story and create new space for the good stuff!

Forgiveness IS...

* The PEACE you feel when you let go of your grievance story.
* IT'S FOR YOU and not the offender.
* Is taking back YOUR POWER.
* Is taking responsibility for how you feel.
* Is about your HEALING and not about the people who hurt you.
* Is a trainable skill just like learning to throw a baseball.
* It helps you get control over your feelings.
* Can improve your mental and physical health.
* Is becoming a hero instead of a victim.
* Is a choice.

Everyone can learn to forgive.

"Forgiveness is the feeling of peace that emerges as you take your hurt less personally, take responsibility for how you feel, and become a hero instead of a victim in the story you tell. Forgiveness is the experience of peacefulness in the present moment."
DR. FRED LUSKIN
Stanford University Forgiveness Project

Forgiveness is NOT...

* Forgiveness is **NOT** accepting unkindness.
* Forgiveness is **NOT** forgetting that something painful happened.
* Forgiveness is **NOT** excusing poor behavior.
* Forgiveness does **NOT** have to be an otherworldly or religious experience.
* Forgiveness is **NOT** denying or minimizing your hurt.
* Forgiveness does **NOT** mean the events were your fault just because you take responsibility for your feelings.
* Forgiveness does **NOT** mean you give up having feelings.

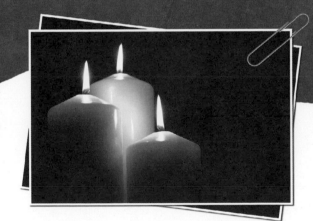

Forgiveness is NOT reconciliation where you need to rebuild a relationship with the person who hurt you. Forgiveness means you make peace with the hurtful event of your past and no longer spend most of your time blaming the experience on the offender.

You have a choice - you can either move on from the relationship or if you feel it's worth it, you might decide to give the person who hurt you another chance.

That choice is totally up to you!

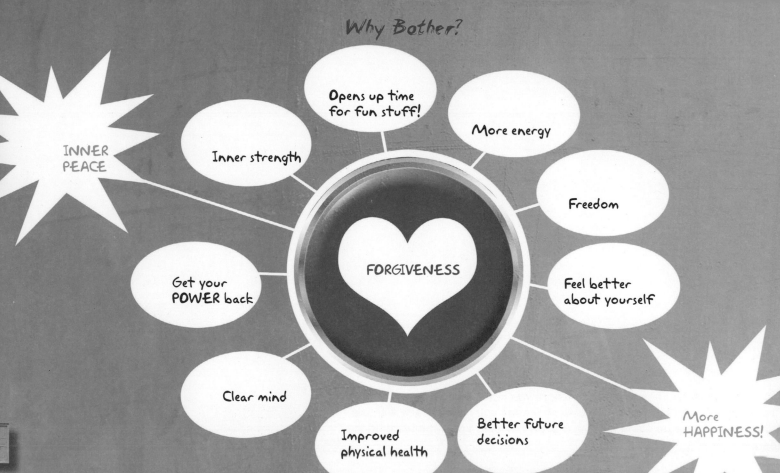

Opens up time for fun stuff!

More energy

INNER PEACE

Inner strength

Freedom

FORGIVENESS

Get your POWER back

Feel better about yourself

Clear mind

Improved physical health

Better future decisions

More HAPPINESS!

When we look closely enough we might realize that the hurt is from our past, which we know we cannot change, while our grievance story is in the present... which we can change. Yes, we have been hurt before, but we can decide how long that hurt will last. When we make the choice to let go of the hurt that is imprisoning and exhausting us, we are faced with so many more opportunities for joy, energy and time with people we care about. And then a funny thing happens... we often feel happier! Why? Well there is a sense of inner peace and inner strength that comes with the decision to take our power back out of the hands of the person who hurt us. When we know that we are the only ones who have power over how we feel, rather than people around us... we feel a new sense of comfort and strength about our lives... even when we're faced with challenges.

134

Rewriting my Story

Many of our hurts come from the ways we believe others should act. What expectations have you established for others? Are these expectations so high that others have no option but to fail?

What grievance story is occupying precious space in your mind? How can you rewrite so it's a story of survival rather than victimhood? How can you get your power back?

Try It...
Are you ready to forgive?
1. Know what your feelings are about what happened.
2. Be clear about the action that wronged you.
3. Share your experience with at least one or two trusted people.
4. Don't forget the good things in your life.

135

What do I NOW know about happiness?
How can I put this into action in my life?

Checking back in:

Ways of Caring (or not):

Disconnect (APATHY): We don't care.

Over-connect (SYMPATHY): We get too attached to someone else's pain.

Connect (EMPATHY): We recognize someone else's pain, but we can maintain our own feelings.

The best way to help others is through empathy.

Before you feel motivated to do something to help someone in need (Compassion in Action), you need to recognize their pain (Empathy).

We won't be able to extend compassion to others until we share it with ourselves first (Self-Compassion).

A good way we can show compassion for others is through compassionate communication (by honestly expressing our needs and listening deeply to others' needs).

Compassion is also about acceptance of others, finding out what's below the surface and learning more about our differences (diversity consciousness).

Forgiveness, a powerful and courageous way to show compassion, is about finding peace and getting our power back. It's about being a survivor not a victim.

VI

INTERDEPENDENCE

"We are all connected – what affects one, affects all in the web of life called Earth"

-Chief Seattle

What Is Interdependence?

Although the word interdependent might be a new term to some of us, if we look closely, we recognize a word that many of us are familiar with: dependent.

In our human experience, this is a term we can all relate to, particularly in the first few years of our lives. From the moment we are born, we depend on others:

- As babies we rely on our caregivers for food, physical care & love.
- Our very survival depends on these acts of kindness!
- As toddlers, other people help us choose what to eat & what to wear.

As we grow up, we develop skills and strengths that allow us to live more independently. We rely less on others and more on ourselves as we begin to make our own choices:

- We choose our friends & the food we eat.
- We decide how we spend our free time.

As we gain more independence with age, our social needs change and need human interaction! Whether we are hanging out with friends, spending time with family, or even just brushing past someone on the street, we connect with people in our environment in some way, each and every day. This means that we rely on each other on some level (resources, emotional support and happiness).

The reality is...

whether we like it or not, we are all interconnected and interdependent. Like the links in a chain, each of our choices and interactions with others are connected to everyone's happiness.

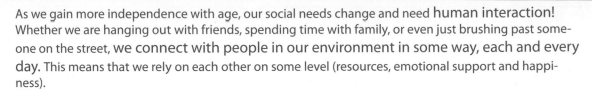

INTERDEPENDENT

We can all depend on each other for the gifts we offer...
We can share our strenghts when the other is weak. I'll teach you math and you can help me write.
Real happiness is about sharing my gifts with you.
Your happiness is my happiness.

INDEPENDENT

We can stand alone...
I'm self-sufficient.
I don't need anyone.
I can survive on my own.
I'm in control of my happiness.

DEPENDENT

We sometimes depend on each other...
Kids depend on parents for shelter, food, & love.
Students depend on teachers for education. We depend on our friends for encouragement.
I depend on others for my happiness.

CO-DEPENDENT

Sometimes we depend too much...
I'd be lost and unhappy without you.
You'd be lost and unhappy without me.

139

Reflecting on My Intentions

Do you agree with these definitions? What is your understanding of the terms dependence, independence, interdependence?

Look at the relationships in your own life. Who do you depend on? How do these relationships affect your happiness? Are they empowering or disempowering?

How do you honor your need for being who you are (independent)? How do you take responsibility for being part of a greater whole where others are relying on you (interdependence)?

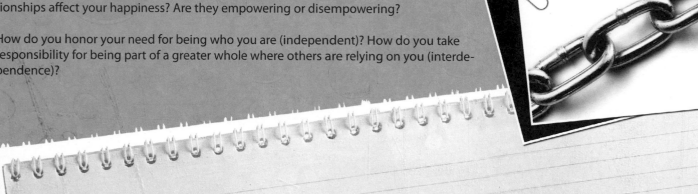

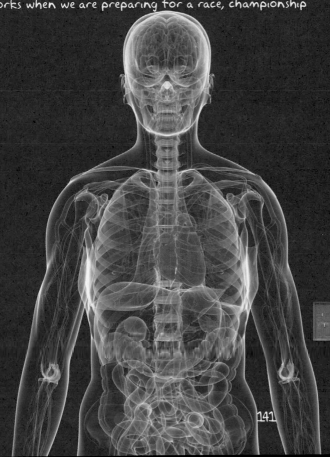

Interdependence: A System of Connected Parts

Another way we can understand interdependence and how it shows up in our lives is to think of it as a human body system. Like any system, it is made up of many different parts that work together towards a common goal. In the case of our bodies, the millions of parts, both large (organ systems) and invisible to the eye (cells), are working together towards the same goal: our health and well-being. Our health depends on how well our system is running and how each part is fulfilling its unique role and contributing to the whole. If one part fails to complete its role, the whole system fails. In this way, each part of our human body is interdependent on one another.

Let's take a look: Here is how our system works when we are preparing for a race, championship game, or performance...

What would happen if one of these systems failed?

Respiratory System: The lungs expand to let more oxygen into the body.

Circular System: The heart pumps more blood (& oxygen) throughout the body.

Nervous System: The control center (brain) gets our other systems ready!

Endocrine System: Adrenaline is released so we are totally alert & ready!

Digestive System: Digestion slows down so our body can focus on performing.

141

The Many Layers of Inter-dependence in Our Lives

"When we try to pick out anything by itself, we find it hitched to everything else in the universe."
JOHN MUIR

Within Each of Us

Our thoughts, feelings, and actions are all connected to each other. For example: even a slight change in a thought can impact how we feel and what we choose to do.

What connections do you notice?

Within Others

Whether we like it or not, we interact with other people all the time. How we interact (verbally and non-verbally) with others (family, friends, classmates, and strangers) affects each of our lives and experiences of happiness.

What effect do your choices have on others?

With Our Natural Environment

Everyday, we are interacting with our environment (nature, animals, plants, food, natural resources) and leaving lasting footprints.

What kind of footprints are you leaving in our world?

142

Just as the physical parts of our bodies (muscles, lungs, heart...) work like a system with each part affecting the others, the same goes with the things which are not so physical our thoughts and feelings. As we learned in Chapter III, how we THINK, FEEL, AND ACT (or REACT) are connected to each other like gears. As one part gets moving, it sets the others in motion too.

For example, let's consider what might happen to how we think, feel, and act when we don't get enough sleep!

School can be stressful and it doesn't stop there. The more stressed I get, the worse I do at school. Stress doesn't help the happiness factor either! It's quite the cycle...

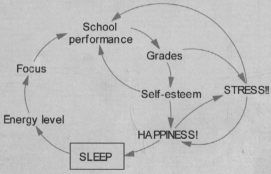

School
performance

Grades

Focus

Self-esteem

STRESS!!

Energy level

HAPPINESS!

SLEEP

Sometimes a lack of sleep will really send a shockwave throughout your day!

And the cycle continues...
How can we break the cy-

143

Tracking My Inner Workings

Let's figure out how this interdependence phenomenon works! Track as much as you can about your day, or if it's too much, just try this for an hour: What did you eat? What did you drink? What actions did you take? What were you thinking? What were you feeling (physically and emotionally)? Record your observations in the right column below. Take a look at the example on the left to guide you: Start by making connections between two choices you made (relationships). Did one choice affect another? Then try making a "Causal Loop Diagram" with all of your choices and see if you can make a whole bunch of connections. Try to include things that can "increase" or "decrease" (e.g., hunger can increase or decrease. It can go either way).

Have fun. There are no wrong or right ways to do this. It's just about noticing the relationships in your own life!

Example:

Relationships

Hungry → Cranky

Cranky → Fight with friend

Fight with friend → Felt guilty

Felt guilty → Ate bag of chips

Ate bag of chips → Sick to my stomach

Casual Loop Diagram

144

Interdependence: Others!

Have you ever heard of the phrase, "What goes around comes around?" It means that for every action there is an effect. For example, if you are friendly and compassionate towards others, you will likely experience more friendship and compassion from others in your own life (even if sometimes it takes longer than we wish). Basically, the choices we make not only impact our own lives and experience of happiness, but others' too.

What kind of choices are you making? How do you think they affect other people's happiness and ultimately your own happiness?

Think about it...

FAMILY & FRIENDS

→ What's your mood when you wake up in the morning? How do you greet others?
→ Do you recognize your siblings or parents needs or struggles? Do you care? What do you do about it?
→ What kind of friend are you? What qualities do you bring to your friendships?

STRANGERS

How do you interact with others, especially people you don't know or might not ever see again? Do you respect them and look them in the eye? Do you smile? When you are buying something, do you acknowledge the person serving you? Do you say thank you?
How do you treat people with special needs: the elderly, people with disabilities, pregnant mothers, the awkward student at school?

Our Journey

We humans are social beings. We come into the world as the result of others actions. We survive here in dependence on others. Whether we like it or not, there is hardly a moment of our lives when we do not benefit from others' activities.
THE DALAI LAMA

Are you happy now? I think we cannot create happiness for ourselves. We'll be happy only when we are able to bring happiness to others. When you interact more with others, your happiness increases.
TENZIN (Tibetan)

The truth is...everything counts. Everything. Everything we do and everything we say. Everything helps or hurts; everything adds to or takes away from someone else.
COUNTEE CULLEN

Checking out My Interactions

There is a constant give & take, ebb & flow, or cause & effect relationship happening between ourselves and the people we interact with. One choice leads to a similar response which leads to another related action and so on. These effects flow both ways–from us and to us. We're grumpy in the morning, so we might affect our sister's morning. A parent yells at us and we might feel resentful the rest of the day. Sometimes our choices leave positive effects and sometimes they don't. Take a look and see what you find out about your interactions (you might even try a causal loop diagram again!):

For one day this week, take a look at the choices you are making in your interactions with others. What kind of response are you getting in return from others (positive or negative)? What was your role in these reactions? If it wasn't so positive, what could you have done differently?

Then take a look at how other's people's choices affect you. Sometimes you have a choice in who you interact with (friends)... and other times you don't (family, teacher, coach). We can choose more supportive friends or realize someone else's mood or struggles are not about us.

→ Who did you interact with?
→ How did you feel interacting with this person? Better? Worse? Neutral?
→ What choices did you make?

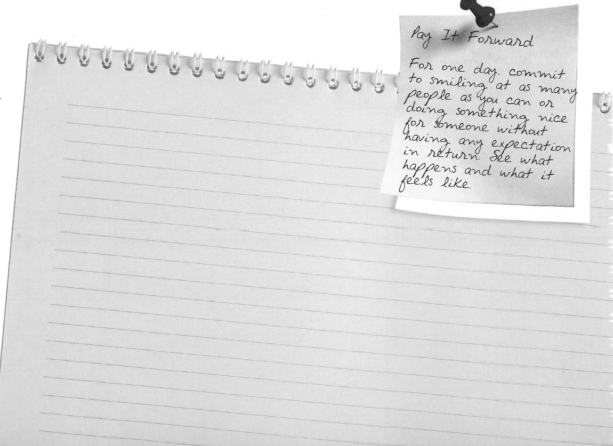

Pay It Forward

For one day, commit to smiling at as many people as you can or doing something nice for someone without having any expectation in return. See what happens and what it feels like.

A Credo For My Relationships with Others
Dr. Thomas Gordon

You and I are in a relationship, which I value and want to keep. Yet each of us is a separate person with unique needs and the right to meet those needs.

When you are having problems meeting your needs I will listen with genuine acceptance so as to facilitate your finding your own solutions instead of depending on mine. I also will respect your right to choose your own beliefs and develop your own values, different though they may be from mine.

However, when your behavior interferes with what I must do to get my own needs met, I will tell you openly and honestly how your behavior affects me, trusting that you respect my needs and feelings enough to try to change the behavior that is unacceptable to me. Also, whenever some behavior of mine is unacceptable to you, I hope you will tell me openly and honestly so I can change my behavior.

At those times when one of us cannot change to meet the other's needs, let us acknowledge that we have a conflict and commit ourselves to resolve each such conflict without either of us resorting to the use of power to win at the expense of the other's losing. I respect your needs, but I also must respect my own. So let us always strive to search for a solution that will be acceptable to both of us. Your needs will be met, and so will mine-neither will lose, both will win.

In this way, you can continue to develop as a person through satisfying your needs, and so can I. Thus, ours can be a healthy relationship in which both of us can strive to become what we are capable of being. And we can continue to relate to each other with mutual respect, love, and peace.

Signed: _____

Interdependence: The Environment!

Beyond our relationships with ourselves and others, we are also directly connected to our natural environment. Just like we depend on our caregivers at birth for our survival, we depend on the natural world for food, water, resources to build our homes, and the air we breathe. This is not, however, a one way relationship; it's an interdependent one…with the health and sustainability of our planet dependent on us to make conscious and respectful choices about how we use the Earth's resources. This interdependent relationship functions like a living system, with each part of our planet (humans, plants, animals, bacteria, rocks, oceans, and atmosphere) shaping and maintaining life on Earth. They call it the Gaia Principle. Whatever happens to one part of the planet affects all the other parts of the planet.

This made sense when people lived off the land:
- Growing crops, raising farm animals, and making crafts
- Living in close contact with the source of their food & their natural surroundings

This natural connection changed as developed nations replaced agriculture with manufacturing…
- Urban living replaced rural living, populations grew, and industry intensified
- People began to see themselves as separate from or even superior to the natural world

Thankfully, with these changing lifestyles and population growth, people finally started to recognize the damage done to our waterways, forests, air and animal populations. We finally realized…the planet can't keep up!

With this new awareness, we began to understand that humankind is not separate from the rest of the natural world. As we harm the well-being of our planet, so too we diminish our own well being: our quality of life suffers, we fight over resources, land is wasted, and resources are too expensive or unavailable. If we want to experience a happiness that can be sustained, then we need to sustain the wellness of the place which offers us this life. It's all about sustainability!

"We do not inherit the world from our parents, we borrow it from our children."
MAHATMA GHANDI

148

Investigating My Relationship with the Planet

Track for a day, or even an hour, what you did and what materials you used (see examples below). Try to identify where each of these materials came from (their source). Then ask yourself how each of the things you did today impacted your happiness. What observations did you make?

Action	Materials	Source	How this action impacts my happiness...
Slept in my bed	Bed frame, sheets, blankets, pillow	Trees, cotton, sheep's wool, goose feathers	There's nothing like the comfort of my bed!!
Ate breakfast	Cereal, orange juice, tea, bowl, spoon, cup, mug	Wheat, sugar, cow's milk, tea leaves, clay, metal, glass	Without breakfast I'd be done for the day.

Observations:

How many of the Earth's resources did I use? What kind of impact might my choices have on the sustainability of our planet? How might my happiness + well-being be affected if these resources were no longer available?

CARETAKING

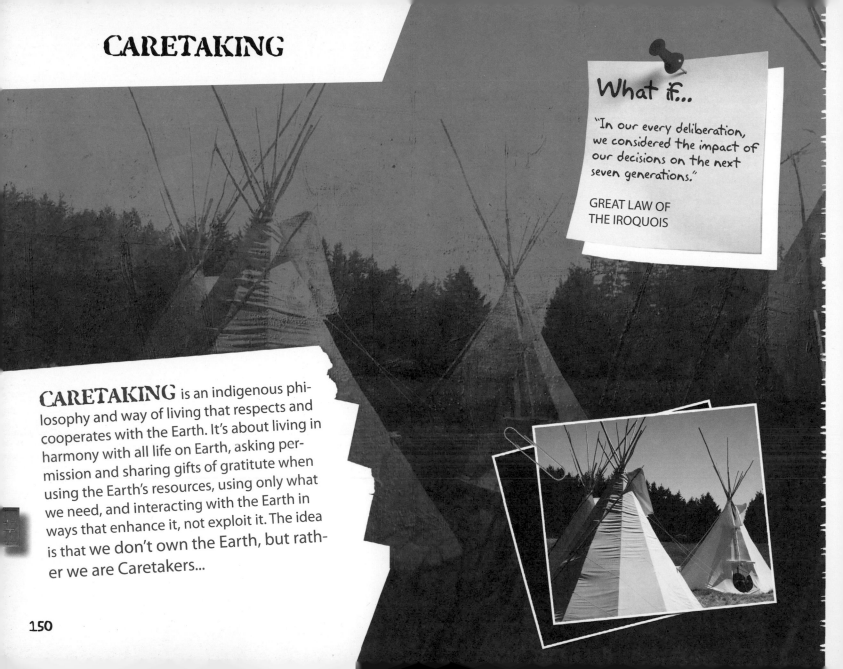

What if...

"In our every deliberation, we considered the impact of our decisions on the next seven generations."

GREAT LAW OF
THE IROQUOIS

CARETAKING is an indigenous philosophy and way of living that respects and cooperates with the Earth. It's about living in harmony with all life on Earth, asking permission and sharing gifts of gratitude when using the Earth's resources, using only what we need, and interacting with the Earth in ways that enhance it, not exploit it. The idea is that we don't own the Earth, but rather we are Caretakers...

Caretaking Legacy
A Native American Story

"You must take things from nature to live, that is a given fact, but it is the way that we take those things and the end results, both immediate and in the future, that make us caretakers."
STALKING WOLF

A Native American nature walk...

→ If we find a stick we like while walking in the forest, we first ask Mother Earth permission.
→ If we disturb the forest during our walk or if we choose to pick up the stick, we leave loose tobacco as a sign of respect and offering of thanks to Mother Earth.

GRANDFATHER

Grandfather said that when the Native American went out to collect a bow stave, it was a very conscious endeavor. First, the Native American had to have an extreme need for the bow stave. Then, the collecting trip would be proceeded by periods of fasting and praying. After all, it was not as simple as just cutting down a tree, for he would be taking the life of his brother. He would then go out onto the land and begin his search.

He was not looking for the solitary saplings that grew straight and tall. Instead, he would search the groves of saplings that were in competition with each other. He knew that in their struggle for soil and sunlight many would die and others would be badly bruised and injured as the years passed. If left alone they would not be strong and healthy. When such a grove was found, he would search it thoroughly, looking for the ideal sapling. It would not be the straightest and tallest. Instead, it would be one that was dying or would eventually be crowded out by the other saplings. He would then ask himself if the land would be left better by removing the sapling. If so, then he would ask what kind of legacy would he leave for his children and grandchildren. Would it be a strong and healthy forest?

Only when those questions were answered in a positive way would he eventually cut the sapling. Even then there must be the prayers of thanksgiving. His was the attitude of the caretaker, helping nature to grow better, stronger, and faster. He could do in a short period of time what would take nature years to accomplish. That was his purpose: to help and nurture creation, not to destroy it.

Roles We Play...

Consumer

→ to expend by use; use up
→ to eat or drink up; devour
→ to use or use up consumer goods

Caretaker

→ takes care of another
→ hired to take care of something (property or a person)

At one end of the spectrum, we can be **consumers**, buying the latest trends & enjoying the immediate gratification of having new things. On the other end, we can be caretakers who consider the health of the planet in our every action. Sometimes we're at one end of the spectrum, other times we hang out at the other and there's the whole range in between. We're not always so extreme.

Can you think of times when you filled each of these roles? Where do you typically hang out (at one end, the other... or somewhere in the middle)?

The Journey of Our Jeans

Have you every directly thought of all the factors that were involved or influenced, either directly or indirectly, by the manufacturing, delivering, & sales of your jeans? Try to trace the many paths your jeans took to land on your lap.

Who, what, where, and at what cost?

153

The Perils of Plastic

Each year, about 500 billion to 1 trillion plastic bags end up as liter.
National Geographic News

Each year, 2.7 million tons of plastic are used to bottle water worldwide.
One World

It costs more to recycle a plastic bag than to produce a new one! Less than 1% of plastic bags are recycled!
Christian Science Monitor Newspaper

Plastic bags photodegrade (not biodegrade), which means that they break down into smaller toxic parts that contaminate soil and waterways, so animals end up eating these toxic parts.
www.reusablebags.com

Oil Oil

1.5 million barrels of oil are used to produce plastic water bottles for America alone = fuel for 100,000 U.S. cars/year.
Earth Policy Institute

Hundreds of thousands of sea turtles, whales, and other marine mammals die every year from eating discarded plastic bags mistaken for food.
www.reusablebags.com

Our Ecological Footprint

Everyone has an Ecological Footprint, it's a figure of how much land and water is needed to support the way we live (the things we consume plus the waste we create). For example, in order for us to live, we require land to grow food and trees, hold waste, and produce plants that can absorb the carbon dioxide emissions we create. As of 2001, the Earth has 1.8 hectares (180 acres) of land/water available per person, but we have been using the equivalent of 2.2 hectares (220 acres) per person. It's pretty clear that nature can't keep with up with our demands!

Go to www.myfootprint.org to calculate the size of your footprint!

Did you know?
If you use cloth bags instead of plastic, you save...
- → 6 bags/week
- → 24 bags/month
- → 288 bags/year
- → 22,176 bags/average lifetime
- → If just 1 out of 5 in USA did this, we'd save 1,330,560,000,000 bags over our lifetime.

Bangladesh & Rwanda have banned plastic bags.

China has banned free plastic bags & will save 37 million barrels of oil each year.

What are you going to do to reduce your ecological footprint?

The Millennium Development Goals

The reality is we are all connected to one another and our planet.
Let's choose to make our world a happier place to live!

"We are the first generation that can put an end to extreme poverty around
the world, and we refuse to miss this opportunity."
The Millennium Campaign

Goal 1: Eradicate extreme poverty and hunger.
More than 1 billion people live on less than $1 a day – 238 million of them are young people.

Goal 2: Achieve universal primary education.
115 million children do not attend primary school – three-fifths of them are girls.

Goal 3: Promote gender equality and empower women.
In 2003, women held 15% of the seats in national parliaments.

Goal 4: Reduce child mortality.
In the developing world, 1 child in 10 dies before its fifth birthday compared to 1 in 143 in high-income countries.

Goal 5: Improve maternal health.
Every year more than 500,000 women die from complications from pregnancy and childbirth.

Goal 6: Combat HIV/AIDS and other diseases.
8000 people die every day from AIDS. Malaria infects 500 million people each year and kills more than 1 million annually. Tuberculosis kills 2 million people/year.

Goal 7: Ensure environmental sustainability.
2.4 billion people lack access to toilets. 1.7 billion people live in countries that are water-stressed where the water supply is decreasing faster than it can be replaced.

Goal 8: Develop a global partnership for development.
$900 billion was invested in arms by governments in 2003 alone; $300 billion each year is spent by rich countries to support domestic agricultural producers.

NO EXCUSE 2015

VOICES AGAINST POVERTY

Exploring My Part

If anything, we have learned that we are not living in isolation. We can choose to close our eyes to what's going on in the world and not care, or we can choose to do something about it! Is there a Millennium Goal that you connect with? If so, explore it! Find out more and see if there's even one small thing you can do to improve the lives of others or our planet. Every act has an impact, regardless of how insignificant it might seem.

"If you think you're too small to be effective, you've never been in bed with a mosquito."
Betty Reese

23-year-old Nguyen Van Dung spent a month bicycling through Vietnam on a 2,100 km journey meeting young people to raise awareness about the Millennium Development Goals!

What Do I NOW Know about Happiness?

Checking back in...

→ We are all connected to each other like links in a chain.

→ Dependence: I rely on you.

→ Independence: I only rely on myself.

→ Interdependence: We rely on each other.

→ How interdependence shows up in our lives:

→ **Within Us:** Our thoughts, feelings, and actions are all connected to each other.

→ **With Others:** Every choice we make has an impact on other people, just as their choices impact us.

→ **With Our Environment:** Our choices impact the health and sustainability of our planet and our own well-being.

→ We don't own the Earth, we are Caretakers!

→ We always have a choice—we can take responsibility for the role we play in affecting our own happiness, that of others, and the planet.

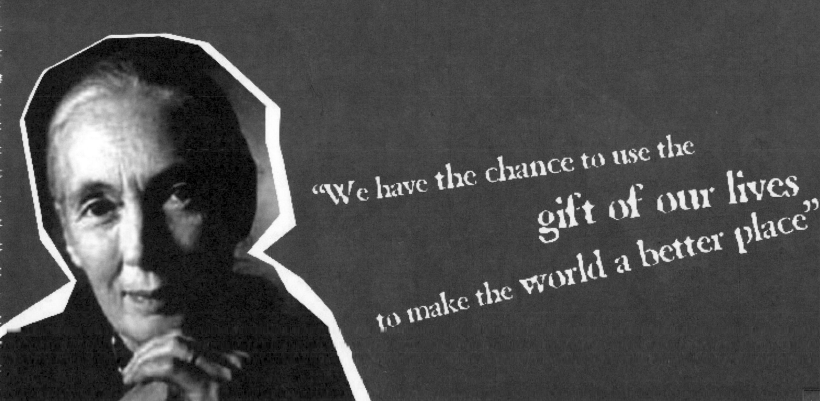

VII

SHARE YOUR GIFTS

"We have the chance to use the *gift of our lives* to make the world a better place"

—Jane Goodall

Opening the Door to Awareness

"They come by and knock on your door with an opportunity. It's your luck if you open the door at the right time."
PRABHA

If we could all just stop for a moment and notice the door that is right in front of us at any given moment...the door to awareness-of who we are in the world, the choices we make, and how they are each connected to our happiness. If we choose to open it, then we are opening ourselves up to an opportunity-an opportunity to understand our role in creating genuine happiness for ourselves and others.

Building Awareness From the Inside Out

When we open the door, what we're really looking at are our relationships, with ourselves and others. The goal of looking at these relationships is to build a new sense of awareness of who we are in the world and what brings us lasting happiness. Many of us began this journey looking outside of ourselves or to our relationships with others to find happiness. Throughout this journey we've been opening up to the idea that happiness comes from understanding our relationship with ourselves first and then taking that happiness and sharing it with others.

Looking Outside
"OPINIONS"

Looking Inside
"ME"

Living Outside
"WE"

"Can you tell me what makes me happy?"
"Is this the right way?"

"What makes me happy?"
"I need to look within myself."

"My happiness is your happiness."
"How can I support your happiness?"

New Awareness: My Own Happiness

When you take responsibility for your own choices and your own happiness, what do you notice about your life?

(Reflect on the tools: When I focus on the good stuff in my life, other things seem to look better too. Tae kwon do and painting help me feel peaceful).

Take the Armor Off

The Will to Listen

Compassion

We All Have a Story

The Power of Words

Forgiveness

162   Control Anger

Look Below the Surface

New Awareness: My Own Happiness

When you take responsibility for the choices you make and how they impact others, what do you notice about your life? How does considering someone else's happiness impact your happiness?

Example: When I take time to get to know someone (below the surface), I realize they have a story a lot like mine and I feel more connected to him/her. They feel understood, which makes me feel good; when I actually just listen to someone rather than get defensive, things get resolved faster & we're better friends.

Thoughts are Powerful

Zone of Peace

Boomerang Effect

Nourish Yourself

Filling up your Cup

Self-Compassion

Paddle Downstream

Forgiveness

163

Community & IMBUTU

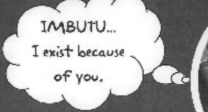

We're also developing a new awareness about our place in community. A social transformation seems to be happening in our world. Millions of individuals and groups are getting in touch with what's meaningful to them and bringing that forward in ways that help others. They are figuring out who they are, what they stand for, and how they can have a positive impact on the world around them!

People are recognizing the value they add to the community!

People in Africa are committed to embracing the unique value each person brings to the whole so everyone may benefit. For them, IMBUTU is expressed throughout the community, which means "I exist because of you." It's as though you breathe life into everyone you encounter and help them uncover the talents and strengths they were born with. As Sobonfu Some, indigenous African wisdom carrier, tells us, community is about creating a safe and trusting place to support the unique GIFTS in each individual. By honoring and continually validating these gifts, each individual becomes a master at what he/she loves and offers a great gift to the community. In this way, everyone thrives!

the community is a puzzle with everyone contributing their own, unique, irreplaceable piece. If we lose even one piece, we can't complete the puzzle.

Finding Happiness...Sharing My Piece

"It is one of the most beautiful compensations in life...that no man can sincerely try to help another without helping himself."
RALPH WALDO EMERSON

Compassion

Spend some quality time with an elderly neighbor once a month.

Athletic

Teach a disadvantaged kid how to play your sport.

Environmental

Take the Ecological Footprint Quiz www.footprintnetwork.org, tell others about it, and give them ideas to make change.

Funny

Visit a children's hospital once in and a while to brighten the spirits of sick kids.

We ALL have a piece of the puzzle. It is a gift, a talent, or a way of being that makes us feel TOTALLY ALIVE!! Not only does this gift bring joy to our own lives, but when shared with others, it can bring great happiness to the community around us. We CAN make a difference in our world! With a new awareness about who we are, mixed with some compassion, we can tap into our gifts and use them for the greater good. And the best part is that WE become happier as a result!

Awareness + Compassion in Action = MORE HAPPINESS

Finding My Piece

What are your gifts, the thing(s) that make you feel totally alive?

Check the ideas below to see if you find anything that sparks an interest. To find out what your strengths are, take the "Signature Strengths Quiz" at www.authentichappiness.com. You might be surprised! Quiz or no quiz, use this space to reflect on what's meaningful to you.

Appreciation of beauty & excellence
Kindness
Justice
Love of learning
Honesty
Leadership
Spirituality
Teamwork
Critical thinking
Wisdom
Curiosity
Social intelligence/Relationships
Enthusiasm
Courage
Capacity to love & be loved
Creativity
Gratitude
Self-discipline
Perseverance
Caution
Forgiveness
Humor
Hope
Modesty

Our Paths to Happiness

These young people recognized a social problem – something unfair – and organized people and events to change these problems. They figured out what they stood for what gifts they could offer and took action. We call them Social Entrepreneurs!

At 12 years old, Zach Hunter learned about Harriet Tubman, a slave who helped in the Underground Railway. Horrified by slavery, he told his mom that he would not stand for slavery if he lived in those times. His mom told him that he is living in the same time – slavery still exists today! Shocked, Zach knew he had to help out. He started a campaign recognizing that most people he knew didn't have large amounts of money to donate. So, instead, he asked people for loose change - the money that had in their cars, pockets, or at home. His campaign has raised thousands of dollars and continues even today!

Source: http://www.cbn.com/700club/guests/bios/Zach_Hunter_122107.aspx

Nandie Ooosthuizen grew up in South Africa and learned about the millions of adults and children in Sudan who have been killed by their government. Many of the Sudan people seek safety and refuge -- any way to escape the violence from their government. Horrified, Nandie began a Save Sudan Project, where she sold "Save Sudan" t-shirts that she created. She has raised over $5,000 for the victims of Sudan to help them escape the violence and plans to continue to teach others about the crisis in Sudan.

Source: http://www.savedarfur.org/page/dashboard/public/Cc9B

Geeta Koli grew up in a slum in India, a place where people believe that a girl's only purpose is to marry, have children, and take care of the family home. Frustrated and believing that everyone deserves an education, male or female, at 18 years old, she set out to change this mentality.

Source: http://www.ashoka.org/examplesyouthventureers

"I don't know what your destiny will be, but one thing I do know: the only ones among you who will be really happy are those who have sought and found how to serve."
ALBERT SCHWEITZER

167

Finding My Path

At 10 years old, living near a rain forest in Costa Rica, Janine Licare noticed the trucks that polluted the air with their black smoke. In 1999, Janine cofounded Kids Saving the Rainforest in order to protect wildlife and their habitat. This organization raises money to protect the rainforest, including the construction of monkey bridges, which are ropes that are above the roads and safe in the forest.

Something to think about

These are people your age, whom saw a problem and decided that they wanted to fix it. Look around you—What do you dream of changing?

"The greatest source of hope for the future is the energy, commitment, and often the courage of young people when they know the problems and are empowered to act. They are changing the world."
JANE GOODALL

The World Needs You

→ Walk, bike, or take public transportation instead of taking a car

→ Unplug electronics when you aren't using it (i.e. unplug your TV when you're not watching your favorite show)

→ Take shorter showers (it saves water and energy!)

→ Recycle all your paper, glass, aluminum, and plastic!

→ Buy recycled products

→ Run the dishwasher only when it's full

→ Use fans instead of an air conditioner

→ Turn the lights off when you're not in the room

→ Plant a garden

→ Eat more local, organic, in-season foods

→ Shop at your local farmer's market

→ Volunteer at your local soup kitchen

→ Volunteer at a nursing home

→ Volunteer at your local animal shelter - help walk dogs or play with the newborn kittens!

→ Create or join a local clothes drive - donate coats that don't fit you or you don't use for people who don't have enough money to buy their own

→ Tutor younger students (Ask your teacher where you can tutor)

→ Read the newspaper, watch the news - find out what's going on in the world!

Our Journey
Our Paths to Happiness

"I realized that pain and sadness are emotions that won't last. They will pass. Like everything, you can get over it. And I'm alive! Happiness is just being here and noticing every detail in my life that brings me joy, especially the small pieces o happiness, like eating a meal."

LUKE

"What touched me most were the orphans at the Gandhi Ashram. They are considered the lowest of the low caste system, the untouchables, but when they sing, their voices are so vibrant, loud, and beatiful. They have been dealt the bad hand in life, but nothing is going to silence them."

NINA

"I learned that you really can't choose the situations you're put in, but you can choose how you deal with them. And the people in the world who are happy are the people who are dealing with their situations well... and the people who are unhappy are the people who aren't."

EMILY

Our Journey
Our Paths to Happiness

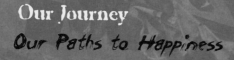

"We are doing everything to be happy, like educating ourselves so that we have a job in the future and enough money to survive in this world. Isn't this too narrow a path for happiness?? Can't we be sharing our goodness and kindness with others and try to be a source of happiness to others?"

YONTEN

"I think the gift is knowing myself and not being somebody else to fit in. I've also been trying to see the beauty in people too."

PRABHA

"Our Tibetan friends are refugees who have all endured terrible hardships. It's almost guaranteed they're not going to see their parents again, and still tney are pretty much the most kind and compassionate people you'd ever meet."

DANIEL

Our Journey
Our Paths to Happiness

"If you think about anything, you're going to start noticing it more, just like happiness. We've been thinking happiness, happiness, happiness. Now, if I'm thinking I'm sad and notice, "Hey I'm not happy!?

JONJI

"It's a dream come true or me to meet people from different countries and share our responsibility to promote world peace and harmony."

DORJI

"When I watch a movie or read a book, I think of ways that it can be ended easily. It's the same with our journey. The journey goes on. You just can't end there. We have to keep rediscovering. The journey to happiness goes on."

MARK

"I was able to do some major reflecting on my lie. By talking to all these people..and seeing how much service brings happiness in their lives, it makes me realize that all the times that I have been teaching, helping, or just being in service, it has brought me so much happiness. I realize this is something I need to focus on in my life."

JOHN NURI

My Path to Happiness

Things have become clear to me: Things about how I have been living, how I want to live, and the kind of person I want to be. I have not always been especially compassionate towards others because I expect people to live at their highest potential. India taught me that **sometimes only compassion and gratefulness are appropriate and that judgments won't get you anywhere.** A great example are the kids that we met in Dharamsala, India. Most of them have left their families behind in Tibet for freedom in India. They have no country, no family, and yet they are some of the happiest, most motivated, and interesting people I've ever met. To me it seems they are this way because they are truly grateful for what they have. **In America we are materially rich, but spiritually devastated.** We put emphasis on products and not on relationships. Seeing the opposite in India really helped me to realize which is more important to me. Since that trip I am the happiest I have ever been. Every day has been a good day because I've realized how much I have to be grateful for. I feel wrong when I complain because I know in my heart that I have nothing to complain about. Thinking like this is very effective for **cultivating compassion,** and my critical mind has changed very dramatically. Now I am critical towards those who are not compassionate to others. We have no right to judge anyone else's situation. And it hurts me when someone is not grateful.

EMILY

A Mother's Reflection of the Journey

Struck by light of insight
of a new way of living,
tracking what brings pain and suffering
and what brings joy and happiness,
they discovered they had choice.

Grateful for the many
aspects of their lives
they had not considered before,
they seemed ill at ease
realizing many did not have such comforts.

Seemingly irreverent
they embarked to a land
where irreverence is unheard of.
They didn't know that
there existed a culture and place
where devotion still ruled
one's life and world view.

Touched in the deepest way
they drew closer to their
hearts-thus themselves-
and they opened
like lotus blossoms
radiating their internal beauty.

My own daughter among them
loving, spirited, and confident
in her gratefulness
found she had more gratitude to express
in her open heartedness,
found she had more love
regardless of circumstance.

THE RIPPLE EFFECT

One person's idea sends a ripple effect across Nigeria, India, America, & the rest of the world...

Randy's Spark! "Everyone deserves to be happy!"

Project Happiness is launched!
Tibetan, Nigerian, & American friends are united & changed forever!

Emmanuel returns home to Nigeria, & with the support of Ward, opens his dream school within 5 months, Creative Minds International Academy.

Shannon, Emily's mom, inspired by Emmanuel's story, visits Emmanuel in Nigeria and brings computers, textbooks, & digital encyclopedias.

Emily, committed to nurturing these lifelong friendships & inspired by her mom's passion, visits Emmanuel in Nigeria to teach his students English.

The Project Happiness team sponsors Emmanuel's school so his students can have access to the Internet and a whole new view of the world.

AND THE RIPPLE CONTINUES...

My Path to Happiness

Along this journey, what have you learned about happiness - your own and that of others? What is YOUR path to happiness? Sketch, write, rap, write a song, dance, create a video - whatever is meaningful to you.

When you're done, post it in your room, carry it in your wallet, listen to it often, share it with others, and most important-**LIVE IT!!**

As you follow your true nature, you inspire others to do the same. You alone can create a ripple effect around the world!

My Credo

I am in charge of my own happiness.

I make the most of today since there will never be another today.

I don't focus on problems; I seek solutions.

I focus on friends and activities that inspire me so that I can inspire others.

I project kindness and I project happiness.

I pay attention to the amount of energy I have and put my best effort in all I do.

I take care of myself in order to take care of others.

"Change your thoughts and you change your world."
Norman Vincent Peale

SO NOW WHAT?

Global Oneness Project www.globalonenessproject.org
Watch inspiring videos about gang life, organic produce, and more!

Seeds of Peace www.seedsofpeace.org
Learn leadership and conflict resolutions skills at these international summer camps where you can meet and befriend people from different cultures!

Taking It Global www.takingitglobal.org
Search for local projects in your community, connect with others who want to create change!

Youth Venture www.genv.net
Get help with your idea!! Find ways to plan events, learn about and start your own youth venture, and become socially and environmentally aware by reading others' experiences!

Global Youth Action Network www.youthlink.org
Connect with more than 10,000 youth activist network groups in more than 100 countries!

Habitat for Humanity www.habitat.org
Join your local habitat and help build a school for a low-income communities!

Tolerance www.tolerance.org
Connect with youth activist groups, find out how to start a "mix it up day" at your school (try to sit with someone different at lunchtime).
Later, share your story about how you've made a difference at your school!

Books for Africa www.booksforafrica.org
Find out how to donate books to children in Africa!

Charity Focus www.charityfocus.org
Find ways to volunteer locally and globally and sign up to receive inspiring quotes and stories through your email.

Volunteer Match www.volunteermatch.org
Search various categories (women, children, poverty, environment, etc.) of interest, then find projects in your area where you can help out!

Help Others www.helpothers.org
Play the "Smile Cards" game and pass them along, or get other great ideas for small acts of kindness.

Ecological Footprint www.myfootprint.org
Calculate your Ecological Footprint and discover ways to be environmentally friendly!

™

www.projecthappiness.com

Our Story

Project Happiness started with a simple idea...how can we be happier as individuals, as a family and as a world community? What is happiness? How do we define it for ourselves and create more of it in our lives when it is so different for each one of us?

Randy's Story

At first, I wanted to have this conversation with my family and friends, particularly my teenagers... and I didn't even know where to start. Happiness is one of those things that's hard to pin down. Because my background is in film, I thought why not connect young people from different countries to explore the nature of happiness? Maybe they would have some answers. That was the moment I founded Project Happiness and our documentary film was born. It features the year long quest of students from India, Nigeria and America as they interview each other, George Lucas, Richard Gere and the Dalai Lama.

Inspired by the students' journey, The Project Happiness Handbook took on a life of its own, eventually including views from world-class leaders in psychology, neuroscience and cross-cultural awareness. Now we had the content, but we had to figure ou how we wanted to share it. It had to be fun, practical and power packed to really transform people's lives. This would require a rare kind of talent. Do you know how sometimes in your life really special people cross your path? The perfect person arrived to bring my vision to life-Maria Lineger. She is a gifted educator, change agent, and writer who has a unique ability to synthesize complex ideas into powerful images. I'll let Maria continue the story...

Maria's Story

When Randy and I met, we immediately had the same vision for the book and it was as though we finished each other's thoughts. It was collaboration at its best! Together with a group of students from the journey, we came up with a design for the book that was personal, provocative and fresh. Using my years of teaching and designing innovative global programs for teens, I gathered the students' reflections and notes, included many empowering ideas Randy and I wanted to share with others, added my own insights and got down to work (for a year)!

As fate would have it, another special person arrived: Ruben Nuñez, the perfect graphic designer. With his empowering and edgy magazine for Hispanic youth, he shared our vision and had the style we were looking for. We were now all our way!

Seven chapters later, it is an honor for us to have had this opportunity and to finally share this journey with you. More happiness is possible. It's a choice, a state, a mindset and a skill. Even if you walk away with just one idea from this book, that idea could change your life.

© Hope Hudson

179

Acknowledgments

Chapter 1: Happiness
Pg 1   His Holiness the Dalai Lama, Ethics for the New Millenium (Riverhead Books,1999), 20.
Pg 8   Ausubel, Nathan. It Could Be Worse: A Treasury of Jewish Folklore (New York: Crown Publishers, 1948), pp. 69–70.
Pg 9   Source: Office Masaru Emoto LLC, ome99999B222.
Pg 15   Tal Ben-Shahar, www.talbenshahar.com.

Chapter 3: Self-Reflection
Pg 44   Adapted from: 6 Seconds, The Emotional Intelligence Network, www.6seconds.org.
Pg 48   Adapted from: Dr. Judith S. Beck, Beck Institute for Cognitive Therapy and Research, www.beckinstitute.org.
Pg 50-51 Adapted from: Dweck, Carol. Mindset: The New Psychology of Success, (New York: Ballantine Books, 2007).
Pg 52   Source: Interview with Richard Davidson, Seattle, Washington, April 13th, 2008.
Pg 56   Adapted from: 6 Seconds, The Emotional Intelligence Network, www.6seconds.org.
Pg 63   Adapted from: Angeles Arrien, Mount Madonna School presentation, fall 2006.
Pg 65   Adapted from: Sobonfu Some, Mount Madonna School presentation, spring 2007.

Chapter 4: Self-Mastery
Pg 74-75 Adapted from: The Art of Will, Robert Assagioli, M.D. Viking Pres 1973.
Pg 89   Adapted from: Kristen Neff, University of Texas at Austin, Self-Compassion. www.self-compassion.org.
Pg 91 Adapted from: The Center for Contemplative Mind in Society, www.contemplativeming.org.
Pg 97 Source: http://www.unicef.org/voy/explore/mdg/explore_2203.html
Pg 100 Adapted from: The Art of Will, Robert Assagioli, M.D. Viking Pres 1973.
Pg 101-03 'Free Parent Effectiveness Training' by Dr. Thomas Gordon, www.gordontraining.com.

Chapter 5: Compassion in Action
Pg 108 Tara Home Training, California.
Pg 118-22 Adapted from: Kristen Neff, Univesity of Texas at Austing, Self-Compassion, www.self-compassion.org.
Pg 125 Adapted from: The Center for Nonviolent Communication www.cnvc.org.
Pg 129-31 Adapted from: Bucher, Richard D. Diveristy Consciousness: Opening our Minds to People, Cultures and Opportunities. New York: Prentice Hall, 2000.
Pg 132-34 Adapted from: Luskin, Dr. Fred. Fore for Good. New York: Harper Collins, 2002.

Chapter 6: Interdependence
Pg 147 Source: Thomas Gordon, Effectiveness Training, www.gordontraining.com.
Pg 151 Source: Brown Jr., Tom. Grandfather. New York: Penguin, 2001.
Pg 154 Source: National Geographic News, http://news.nationalgeographic.com/news/2003/09/0902_030902_plasticbags.html
Pg 155 Source: The Happy Planet Index, http://www.happyplanetindex.org/ecological-footprint.htm, http://www.reusablebags.com/facts.php CNN.com/asia January 9, 2008
Pg 156 Source: The Millennium Campaign, http://cyberschoolbus.un.org/mdgs or visit www.millenniumcampaign.org

Chapter 7: Share your Gift
Pg 168 Source: http://www.kidssavingtherainforest.org.